Editorial Project Manager
Lorin Klistoff, M.A.

Editor-in-Chief
Sharon Coan, M.S. Ed.

Illustrator
Blanca Apodaca
Kelly McMahon

Cover Artist
Brenda DiAntonis

Art Manager
Kevin Barnes

Art Director
CJae Froshay

Imaging
James Edward Grace
Rosa C. See

Product Manager
Phil Garcia

Publishers
Mary D. Smith, M.S. Ed.

Book 1

PHONICS

fox

mop
fox
box
dot
sock

Authors

Kathy Dickinson Crane & Kathleen Law

Teacher Created Resources

Teacher Created Resources, Inc.
6421 Industry Way
Westminster, CA 92683
www.teachercreated.com
ISBN-0-7439-3015-0
©2004 Teacher Created Resources, Inc.
Reprinted, 2004
Made in U.S.A.

Table of Contents

Introduction

By definition, phonics emphasizes how spellings are related to speech sounds in systematic ways; simply put, phonics refers to letter-sound relationships. Long considered important by many, research now supports the need for phonics as an element of reading instruction. This workbook, *Phonics: Book 1*, provides practice in phonics skills for beginning readers.

Phonics: Book 1 is part of a three-book series. As the first workbook in this companion series, *Phonics: Book 1* provides practice and review for both phonemic awareness and alphabet skills. It extends this review into an introduction of phonics as it reinforces the sound-symbol relationships within the alphabet.

This workbook has been designed as a tool for additional practice for students moving into reading. Phonemic awareness and alphabet recognition skills are reinforced as students identify pictures beginning with featured sounds. After reviewing consonant sounds, students will work with both short and long vowel sounds. Blends and digraphs will also be explored. With the support of picture clues, students will use phonics to begin reading.

The ability to read is critical to an effective education. The activities in this workbook support the learning process by reviewing important reading skills and by providing an opportunity for independent practice of these reading skills. When used in conjunction with a phonics-based reading program, this workbook will strengthen the learner's ability to read.

UNIT 1
Consonants

Identify Consonant Pairs

Directions: Each uppercase consonant has a matching lowercase letter that shares the same sound. Color each star that contains a matching pair.

Sound of Ss

Directions: *Sun* begins with the sound of **s**. Circle each picture inside the sun that begins with the sound of **s**.

Sound of Tt

Directions: *Turtle* begins with the sound of **t**. Color each turtle that contains a picture that begins with the sound of **t**.

Sound of Bb

Bb

Directions: *Butterfly* begins with the sound of **b**. Circle each picture on the wings of the butterfly that begins with the sound of **b**.

Sounds of Ss, Tt, and Bb

 $\underline{\underline{S}s}$ $\underline{\underline{T}t}$  $\underline{B}b$

Directions: Say the name of each picture. Write the correct letter pair under the picture that represents its beginning sound.

1.

2.

3.

4.

5.

6.

7.

8.

9.

10.

11.

12.

Sound of Hh

Directions: House begins with the sound of **h**. Color each picture whose name begins with the sound of **h**.

Sound of Mm

Directions: *Mitten* begins with the sound of **m**. Circle each picture whose name begins with the sound of **m**.

Sound of Kk

Directions: *Kite* begins with the sound of **k**. Circle each picture whose name begins with the sound of **k**.

Sounds of Hh, Mm, and Kk

Directions: Say the name of each picture. Write the letter pair under the picture that represents its beginning sound.

1. H h

2. M m

3. K k

4.

5.

6.

7.

8.

9.

10.

11.

12.

Sound of Jj

Directions: *Jellybean* begins with the sound of **j**. Inside the jellybean frame, draw two pictures that begin with the **j** sound.

Sound of Ff

Directions: *Football* begins with the sound of **f**. Color each picture that begins with the **f** sound.

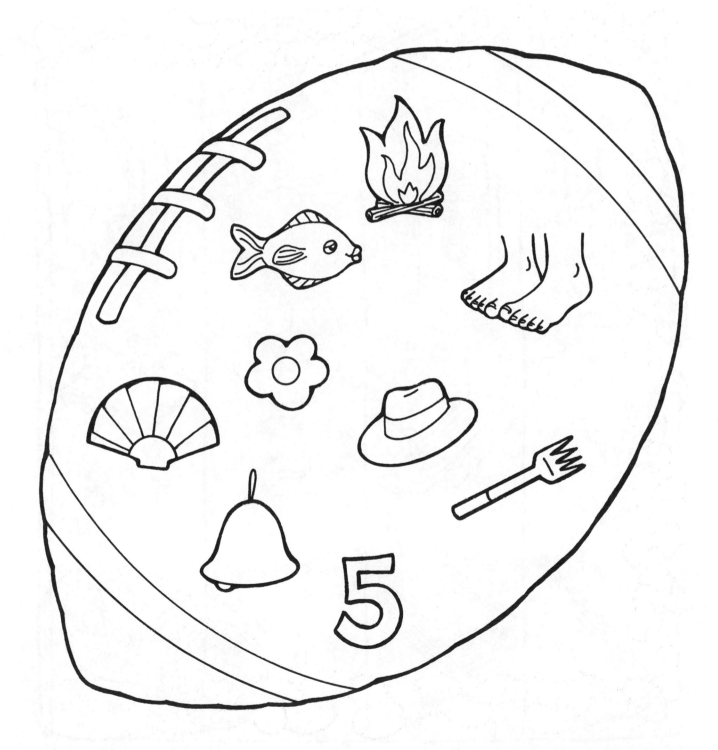

Sound of Gg

Directions: *Gate* begins with the sound of **g**. Circle each picture that begins with the **g** sound.

Sounds of Jj, Ff, and Gg

 J j F f  G g

Directions: Say the name of each picture. Write the correct letter pair under the picture that represents its beginning sound.

Sound of Ll

Directions: *Leaf* begins with the sound of **l**. Circle each picture inside the leaf whose name begins with the sound of **l**.

Sound of Dd

Directions: *Door* begins with the sound of **d**. Color each door whose picture has a name that begins with the sound of **d**.

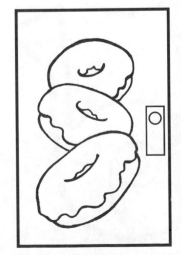 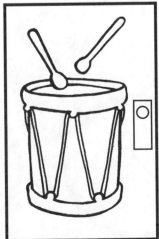 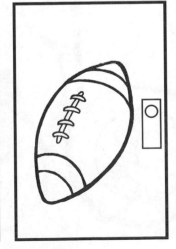 

Sound of Nn

Nn

Directions: *Note* begins with the sound of **n**. Color each note that has a picture whose name begins with the sound of **n**.

Sounds of Ll, Dd, and Nn

Directions: Say the name of each picture. Write the letter pair under the picture that represents its beginning sound.

1. Ll

2. Dd

3. Nn

4.

5.

6.

7.

8.

9.

10.

11.

12.

Identify Consonant Pairs

Directions: Be a detective! Color the magnifying glass that has the matching uppercase and lowercase letters.

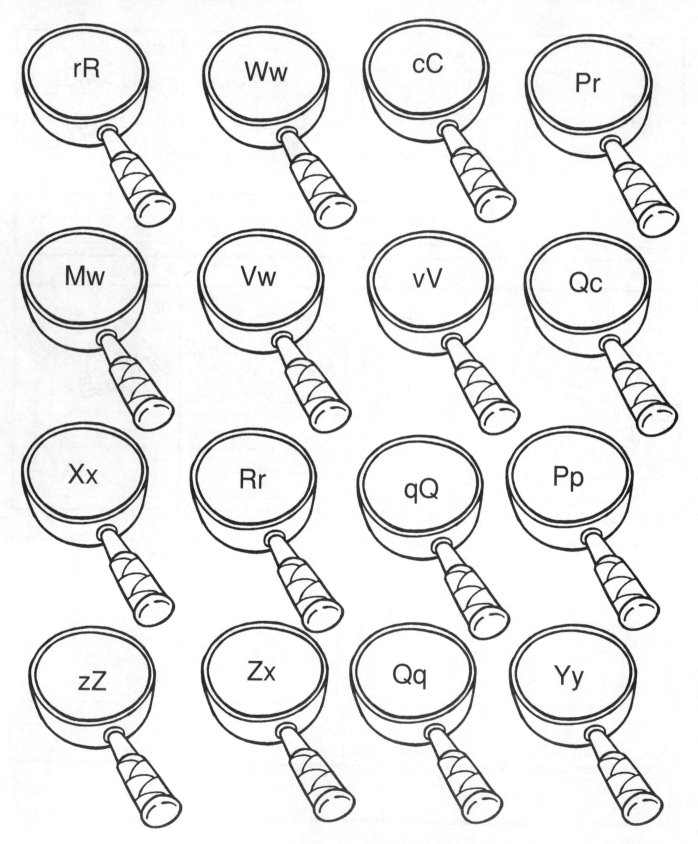

rR   Ww   cC   Pr

Mw   Vw   vV   Qc

Xx   Rr   qQ   Pp

zZ   Zx   Qq   Yy

Sound of Ww

Directions: *Window* begins with the sound of **w**. Circle each picture that begins with the **w** sound.

Sound of Cc

Directions: *Cone* begins with the hard sound of **c**. Color each scoop that contains a word that begins with the hard **c** sound.

Sound of Rr

Directions: *Ring* begins with the sound of **r.** Circle each picture inside the ring that begins with the sound of **r.**

Sounds of Ww, Cc, and Rr

 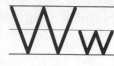 Ww   Cc    Rr

Directions: Say the name of each picture. Write the correct letter pair under the picture that represents its beginning sound.

1. 	2. 	3. 	4. 
_____	_____	_____	_____

5. 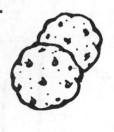	6. 	7. 	8. 
_____	_____	_____	_____

9. 	10.	11. 	12. 
_____	_____	_____	_____

Sound of Pp

P p

Directions: *Pumpkin* begins with the sound of **p**. Circle each picture whose name begins with the sound of **p**.

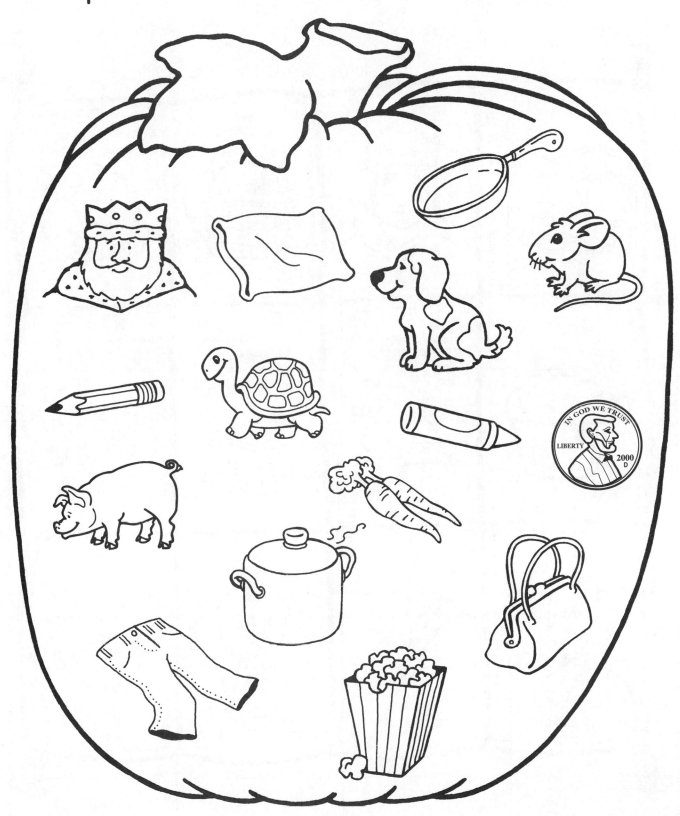

Sound of Qq

Directions: *Quilt* begins with the sound of **q**. Color each square that has a picture that begins with the sound of **q**.

Sound of Vv

Directions: *Valentine* begins with the sound of **v**. Circle each picture whose name begins with the sound of **v**.

Sounds of Pp, Qq, and Vv

Directions: Say the name of each picture. Write the letter pair under the picture that represents its beginning sound.

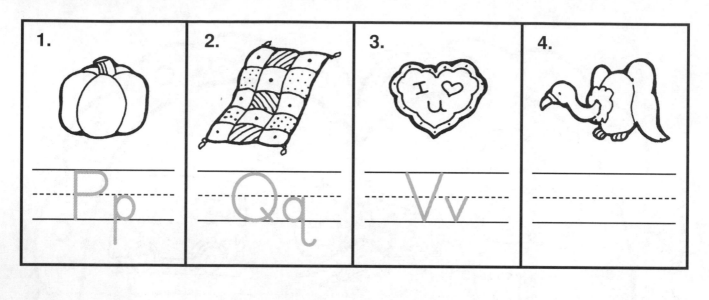

1. Pp

2. Qq

3. Vv

4.

5.

6.

7.

8.

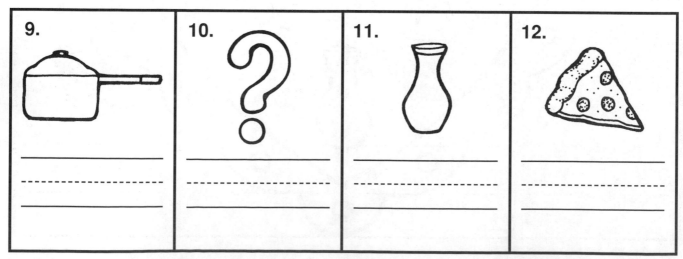

9.

10.

11.

12.

Sound of Xx

Directions: *Fox* ends with the sound of **x**. Circle the pictures that end with the **x** sound.

Directions: Say the name of each picture. Print the missing letter in each word, and then trace the rest of the word.

Sound of Yy

Directions: *Yak* begins with the sound of **y**. Say the name of each picture below and circle the words that begin with the **y** sound.

Directions: Say the name of each picture below. Print the missing letter in each word. Then trace the rest of the word.

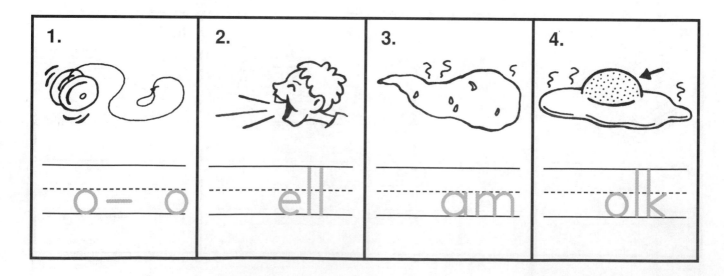

1.	2.	3.	4.
o-o	ell	am	olk

Sound of Zz

Zz

Directions: *Zoo* begins with the sound of **z**. Say the name of each picture below and circle the words that begin with the **z** sound.

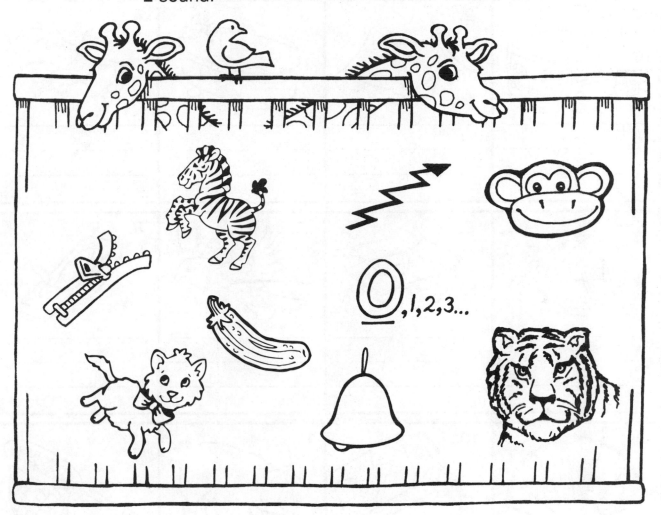

Directions: Say the name of each picture below. Print the missing letter in each word, then trace the rest of the word.

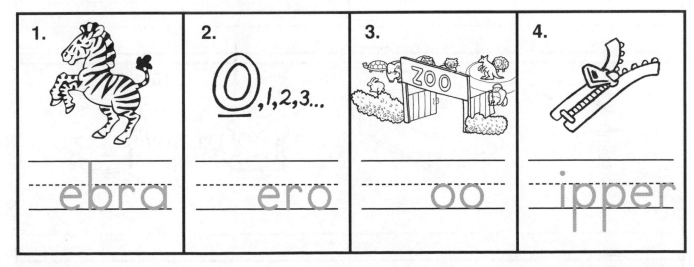

1. ___ebra

2. ___ero

3. ___oo

4. ___ipper

Final Consonants

Directions: Say the name of each picture, listening to the ending sound. Print the letter that is the ending sound.

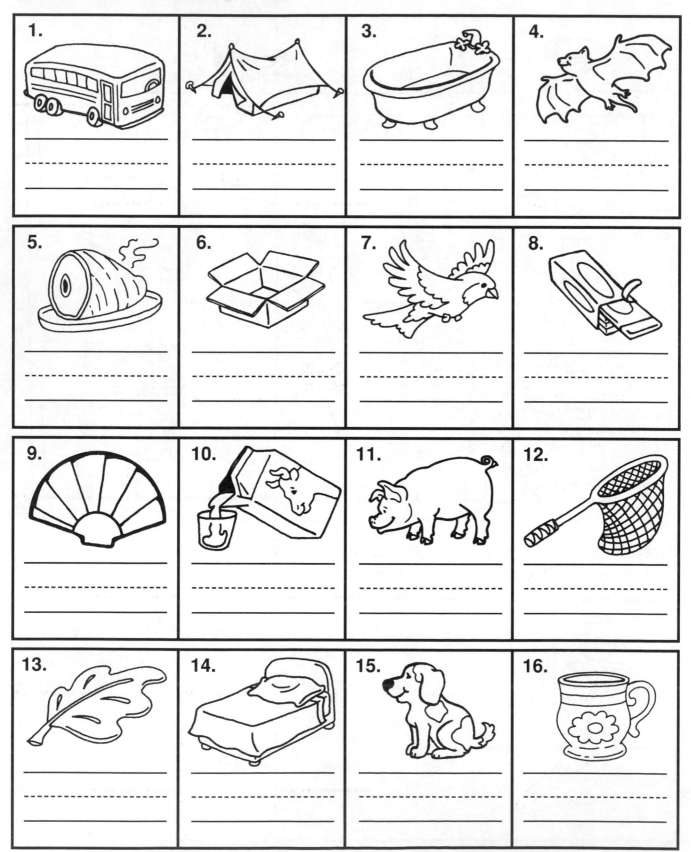

Beginning and Final Consonants

Directions: Say each picture name. Write the letters for the missing beginning and ending sounds. What is the secret message?

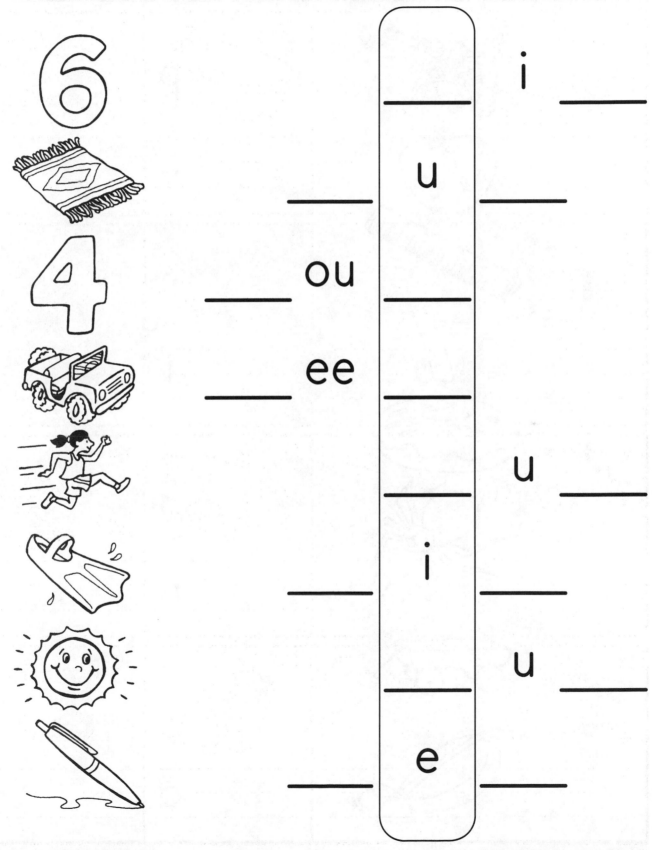

___ i ___

u

___ ou ___

___ ee ___

u

___ u ___

i

___ ___

u

___ u ___

e

___ ___

Medial Consonants

Directions: Draw a line from the picture to the letter that matches its middle sound.

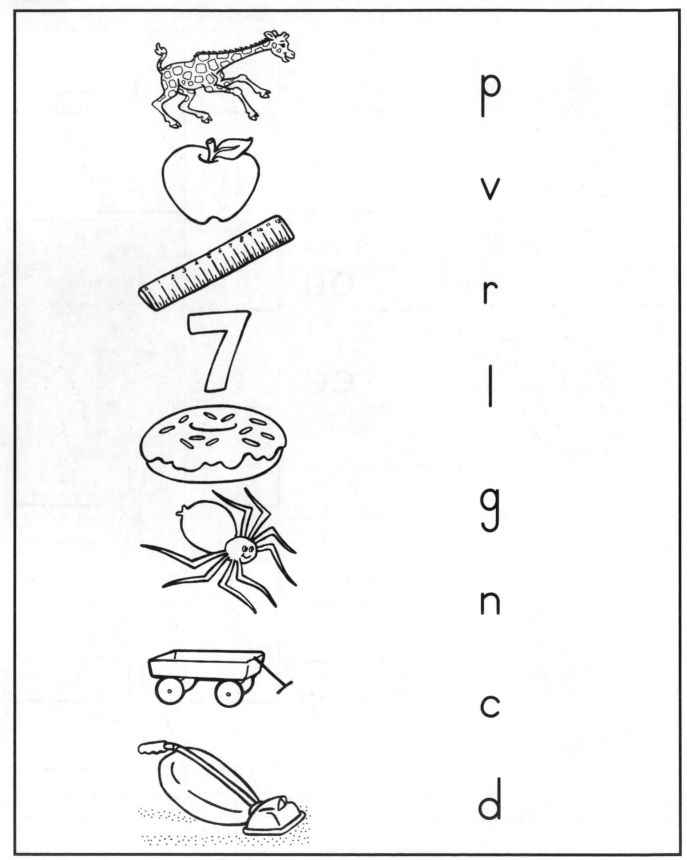

Medial Consonants

Directions: Say each picture name. Print the missing letter or middle sound for each word. Then trace the whole word.

1.  ro __ ot	2.  wa __ er	3.  pa __ er
4.  la __ y	5.  la __ a	6.  ba __ y
7.  hu __ a	8.  wa __ on	9.  ti __ er

Unit Review

Directions: Say the name of each picture. Circle the first, middle, or last letter to show where you hear it in the word.

1.	2.	3.	4.
l l l	t t t	m m m	p p p

5.	6.	7.	8.
x x x	c c c	n n n	b b b

9.	10.	11.	12.
v v v	f f f	d d d	y y y

Unit Review

Directions: Say the name of each picture. Print the letters for the beginning and the ending sound to finish each word.

1. ___ u ___

2. ___ u ___

3. ___ a ___

4. ___ i ___

5. ___ u ___

6. ___ e ___

7. ___ a ___

8. ___ e ___

9. ___ u ___

10. ___ i ___

11. ___ i ___

12. ___ i ___

UNIT 2
Short Vowels

Identify Vowel Pairs

Directions: Which way should you go? Color the signs with the matching pairs to learn your new direction.

Short Aa

Directions: *Apple* has the short sound of **a**. Circle each picture whose name has the short sound of **a**.

Short Aa

Directions: Say the name of each picture. Circle its name.

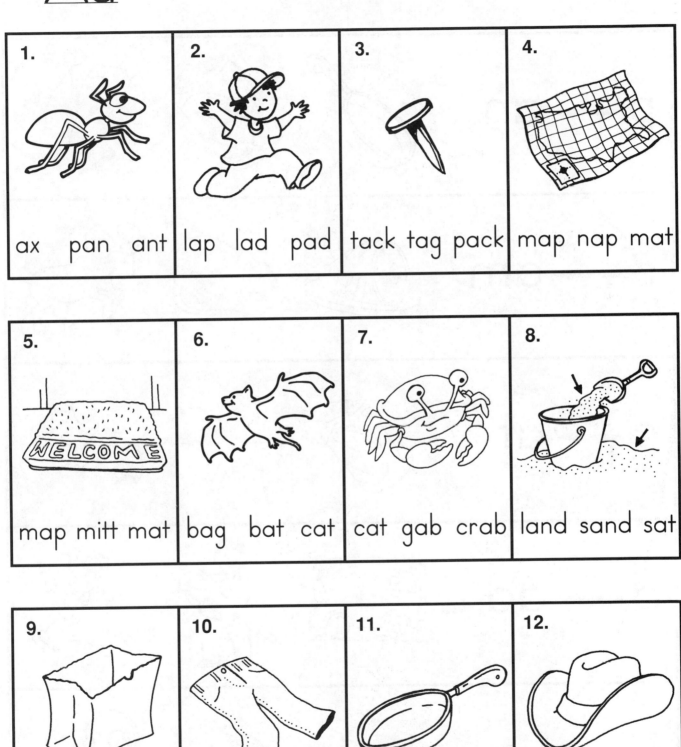

1.	**2.**	**3.**	**4.**
ax pan ant	lap lad pad	tack tag pack	map nap mat
5.	**6.**	**7.**	**8.**
map mitt mat	bag bat cat	cat gab crab	land sand sat
9.	**10.**	**11.**	**12.**
bag bat wag	pad pants ant	pad pan dad	rat ham hat

Short Aa

Directions: Blend the letter sounds together as you say each word. Then color the picture it names.

p ➞ an

r ➞ am

c ➞ at

d ➞ ad

t ➞ ag

Short Aa

Directions: Help the lamb get to school. Draw a line from the lamb to the first word with the short **a** sound. Draw a line to each short **a** word until the lamb is at school!

cat

fan

ten

ant

bun

fad

red

fun

box

rack

pit

hut

at

and

log

lamp

map

dig

SCHOOL

Short Aa

Directions: Look at a sentence. Circle the word that will finish it. Print the word on the line. Use the pictures as clues.

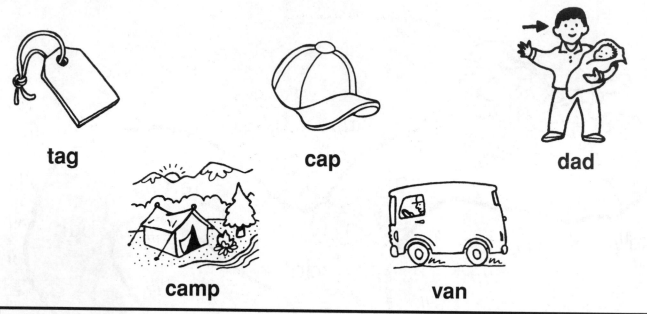

tag   **cap**   **dad**

camp   **van**

1. Dan is in the _____ .	_____	tan van ten
2. He is with his _____ .	_____	dad mad sad
3. On his head, Dan has a _____ .	_____	tap nap cap
4. It has a _____ on it.	_____	tag sat cab
5. Dan will wear the cap at _____ .	_____	can van camp

Short Ii

Ii

Directions: *Igloo* has the short sound of **i**. Circle each picture whose name has the short sound of **i**.

Short Ii

Ii **Directions:** Blend the letter sounds together as you say each word. Then color the picture it names.

s → ick  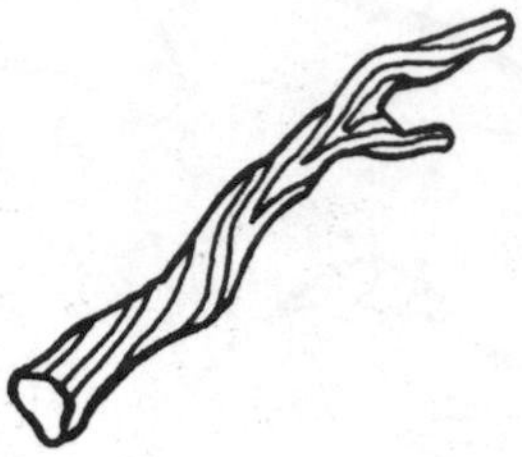 

p → ig   

s → ix   

h → im   

z → ip 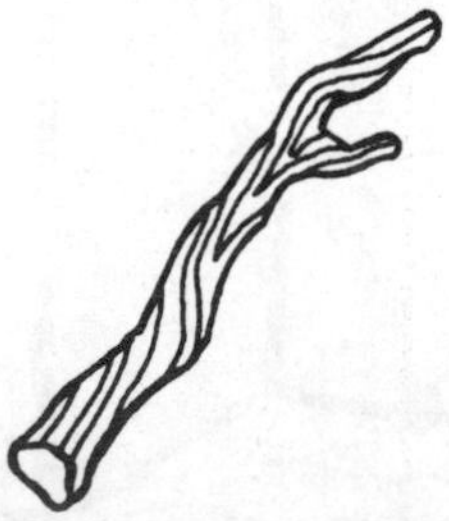  

Short Ii

Ii

Directions: Say the name of each picture. Circle its name.

1. fish   fib   fist
2. rib   bub   bib
3. kiss   kid   lid
4. miss   kid   kiss

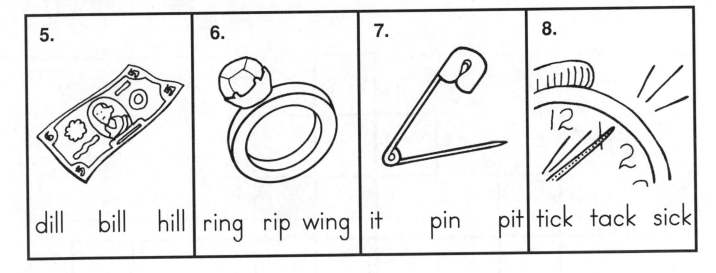

5. dill   bill   hill
6. ring   rip   wing
7. it   pin   pit
8. tick   tack   sick

9. ill   pit   pill
10. sis   hiss   sit
11. dip   dig   fig
12. wit   bin   win

Short Ii

Ii

Directions: Read the words in the box. Print a word in the puzzle to name each picture.

Across →

2   5    6

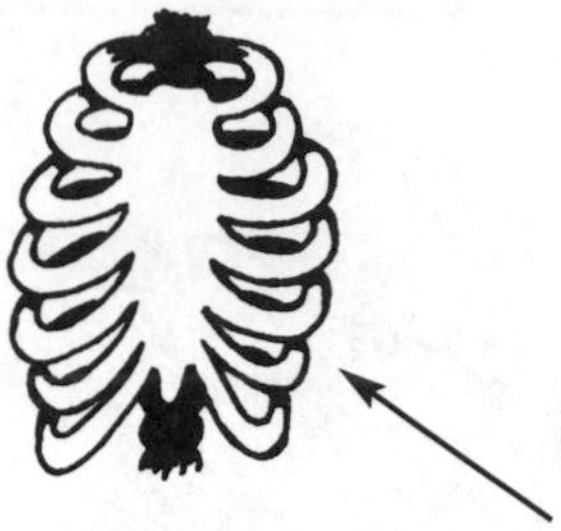

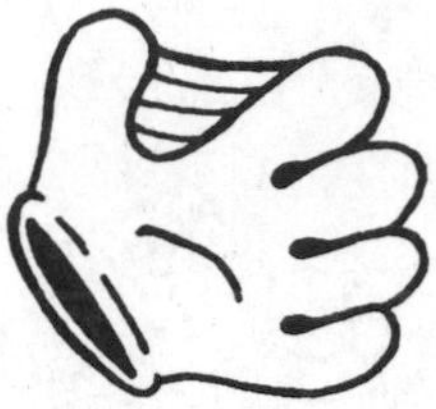

Down ↓

1   3    4

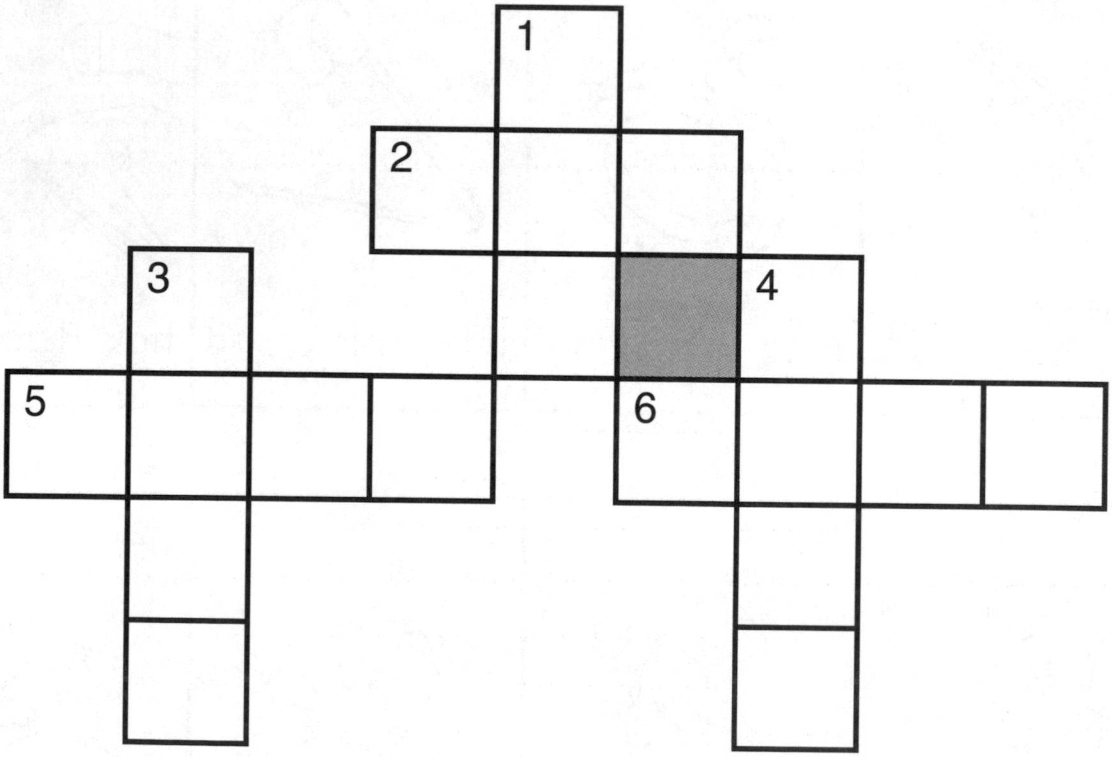

fish   pin   mitt   gift   rib   hill

Short Ii

Directions: Read each sentence. Circle the word that will finish it. Print the word on the line. Use the pictures as clues.

kiss

pig

milk

hill

big

1. Bill is my _____ .	fig dig pig
2. He is _____ .	big bag rig
3. He walked up a _____ .	big hill fill
4. He likes to sip _____ .	bib milk mill
5. I will give him a _____ !	miss rig kiss

Short Aa and Ii Review

Directions: Color the shapes using this key.

Letter **a** and short **a** pictures = purple

Letter **i** and short **i** pictures = green

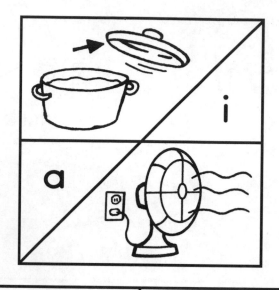

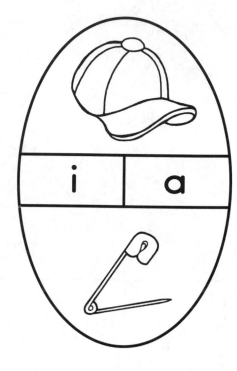

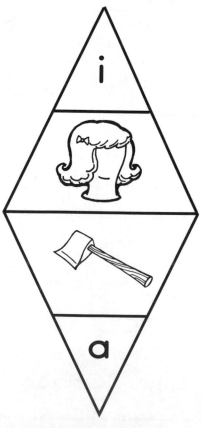

Short Uu

Directions: *Umbrella* has the short sound of **u**. Circle each picture whose name has the short sound of **u**.

Short Uu

 Directions: Say the name of each picture. Circle its name.

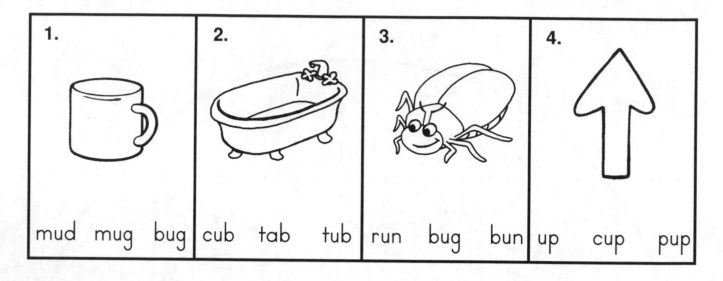

1.	2.	3.	4.
mud mug bug	cub tab tub	run bug bun	up cup pup

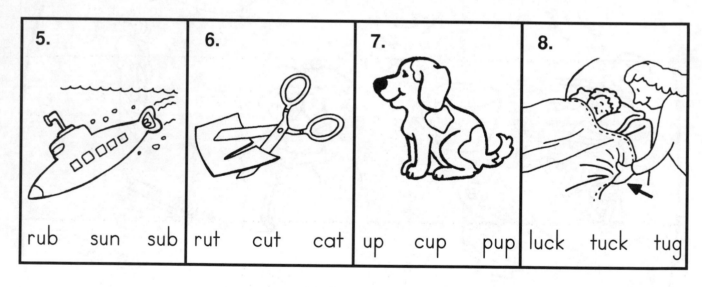

5.	6.	7.	8.
rub sun sub	rut cut cat	up cup pup	luck tuck tug

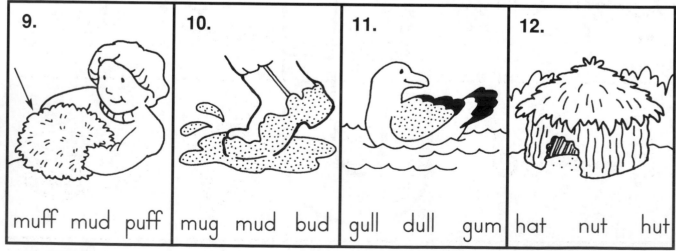

9.	10.	11.	12.
muff mud puff	mug mud bud	gull dull gum	hat nut hut

Short Uu

Directions: Blend the letter sounds together as you say each word. Then color the picture it names.

t → ug

d → uck

c → ut

g → um

b → ud

Short Uu

Directions: Read the words in the bus. Circle each word in the puzzle.

b	d	r	k
u	r	u	g
s	u	n	u
n	m	u	m
h	u	t	x

sun   bus   hut   drum

run   gum   rug   nut

Short Uu

Uu **Directions:** Look at a sentence. Circle the word that will finish it. Print the word on the line. Use the pictures as clues.

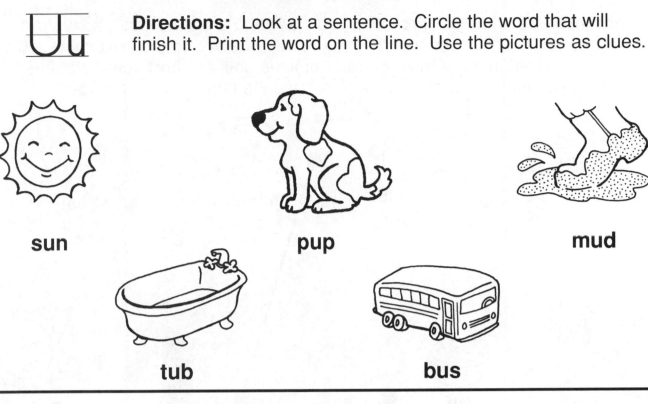

sun   pup   mud

tub   bus

1. I have a _____ _____ .	sup run pup
2. He rides the _____ _____ .	Gus bus rub
3. We run in the _____ _____ .	fun sun tum
4. He dug in the _____ _____ .	bud dull mud
5. I put him in the _____ _____ .	dug tub bub

Short Aa, Ii, and Uu Review

Directions: Begin at the umbrella. Draw a line to a picture that has a short vowel sound. Say the name of the picture. Draw a line to the next short vowel picture. Say the name of the picture. Continue until all short vowel pictures have been connected to make a picture. Use the numbers to help you.

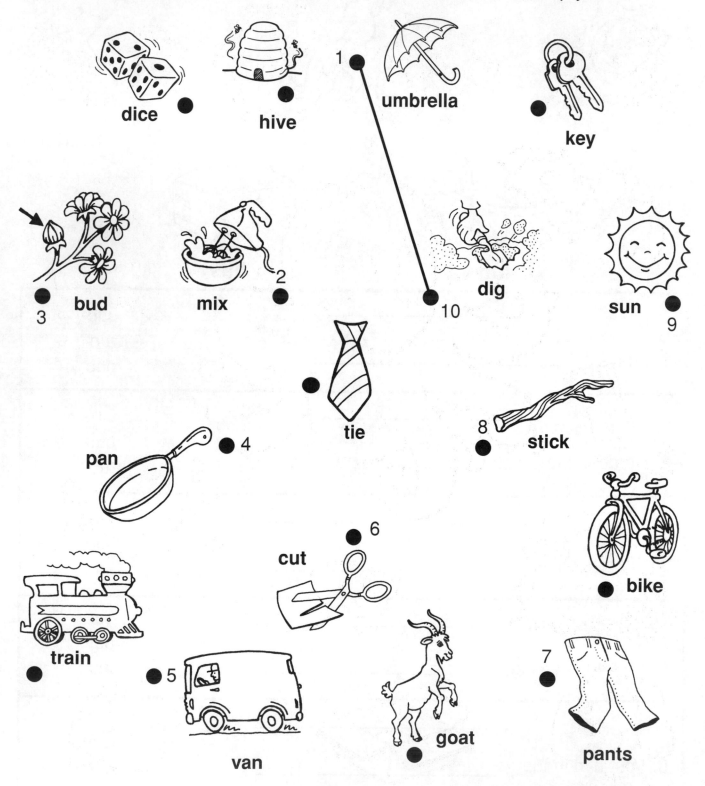

dice

hive

1 umbrella

key

bud
3

mix
2

dig

sun
9

tie

8 stick

pan ● 4

cut 6

bike

train

5 van

goat

7 pants

Short Oo

Directions: Say each picture name. Circle the pictures that contain the short **o** sound as in *octopus*.

Short Oo

Directions: Write the missing **o** in each word. Then draw a line from the word to its matching picture.

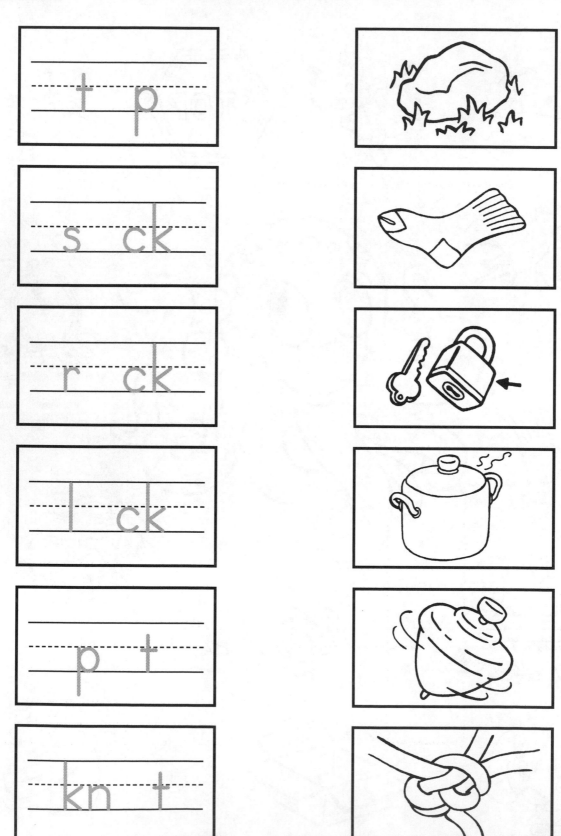

t_p

s_ck

r_ck

l_ck

p_t

kn_t

Short Oo

Directions: Print the missing letters in the boxes to make words that will label each picture.

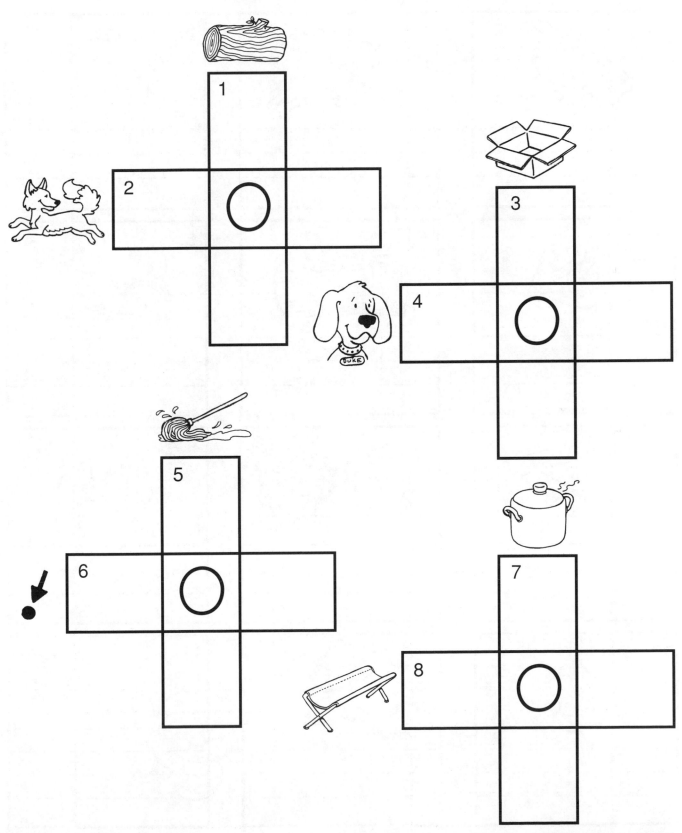

Short Oo

Directions: Say the name of each picture. Write the missing letter for each word. Then trace the whole word.

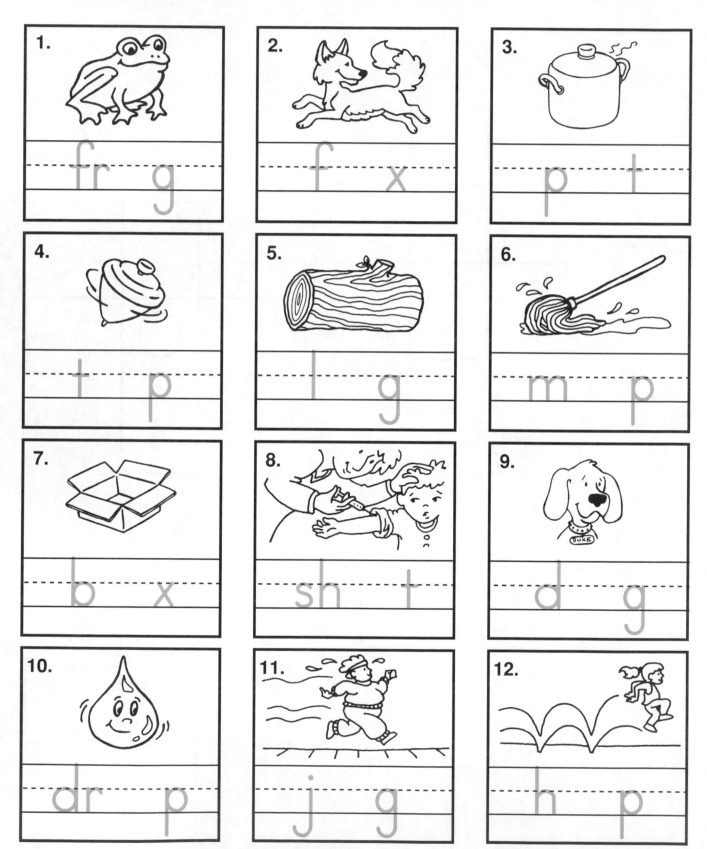

1. fr _ g

2. f _ x

3. p _ t

4. t _ p

5. l _ g

6. m _ p

7. b _ x

8. sh _ t

9. d _ g

10. dr _ p

11. j _ g

12. h _ p

Short Oo

Directions: Say the name of each picture. Write the correct word in the space provided to finish the sentence.

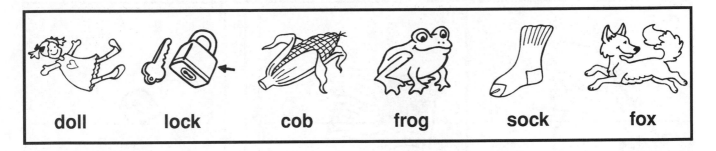

doll   lock   cob   frog   sock   fox

1. The key was in the _____ .

2. The corn was on the _____ .

3. The girl loved her _____ .

4. The _____ was on a log.

Short Aa, Ii, Uu, and Oo Review

Directions: Draw a line from the picture to the letter that matches the short vowel sound.

1. a i o u	2. a i o u	3. a i o u
4. a i o u	5. a i o u	6. a i o u
7. a i o u	8. a i o u	9. a i o u

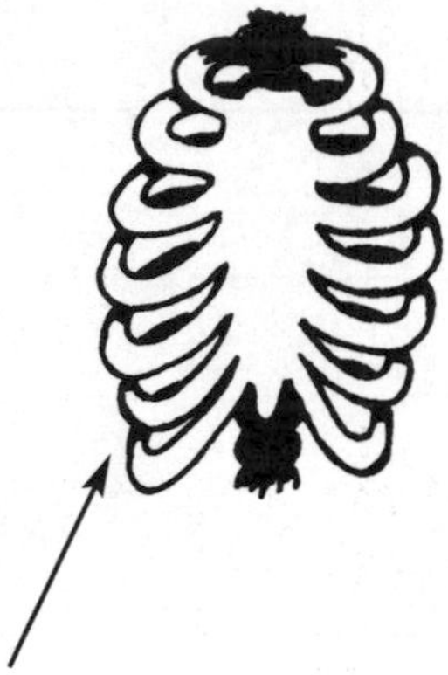

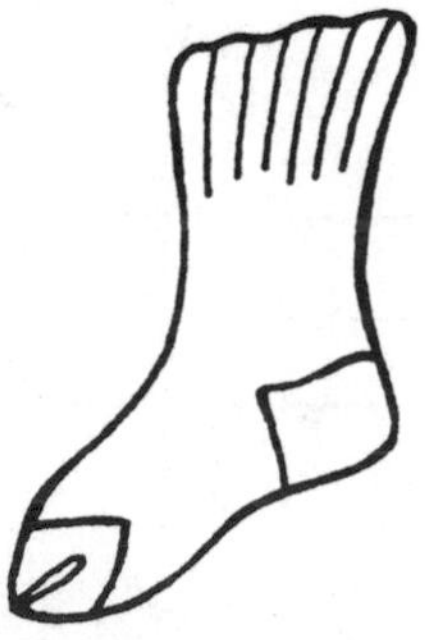

Short Ee

Ee **Directions:** Say the name of each picture. Circle the words that contain the short **e** sound.

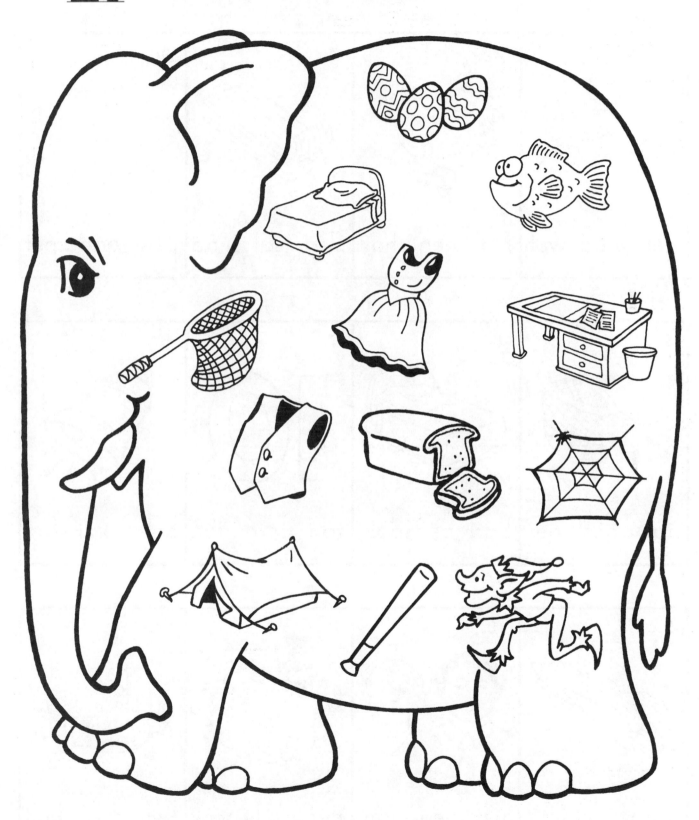

Short Ee

Ee

Directions: Say the name of each picture. Circle the correct word.

1.	2.	3.	4.
web wed wet	net hen hat	sled sat send	pen pan pet

5.	6.	7.	8.
nat not net	bad bed dab	tan ton ten	bell ball lap

9.	10.	11.	12.
jam jar jet	met men map	net nest neck	belt bet bolt

Short Ee

Ee **Directions:** Write the missing **e** in each word. Then draw a line from the word to its matching picture.

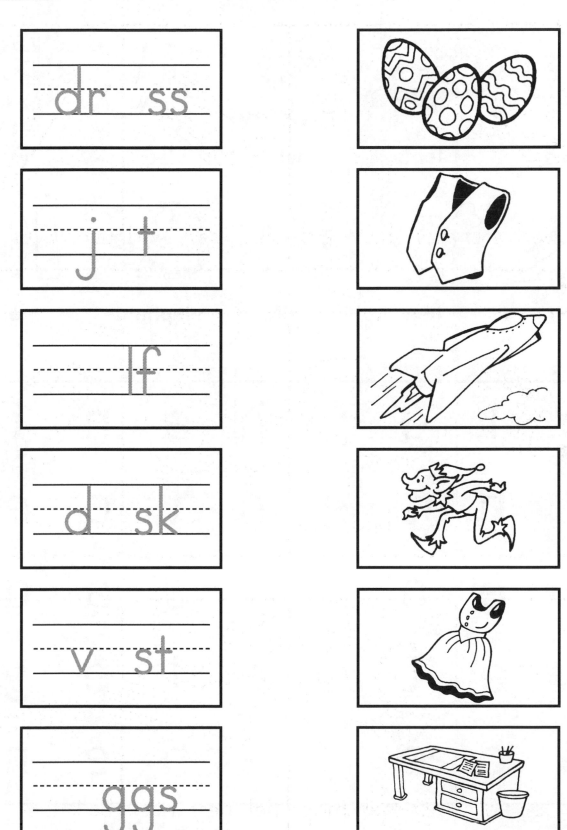

dr__ss

j__t

__lf

d__sk

v__st

__ggs

Short Ee

 Directions: Say the name of each picture. Find and circle the matching word in the puzzle below.

head

tent

pets

leg

wet

pen

hen

elf

elephant

ten

```
e l e p h a n t
l h t e n t e e
f e e t h e a d
w e t s e l e g
e p e n e h e n
```

Short Ee

Ee **Directions:** Circle the word that will finish the sentence below. Then print the word on the line.

1. The elephant is _____ .

wet
dog
cat

2. He is Santa's _____ .

truck
elf
log

3. He writes with a _____ .

hen
ten
pen

4. The _____ is for camping.

dog
ten
tent

5. _____ are good to eat.

Eggs
Pens
Wet

6. A _____ goes very fast.

wet
jet
ten

Short Vowel Review

Directions: Look at the letter in the first column. Say each picture name in that row and circle each picture that contains the letter sound.

Short Vowel Review

Directions: Name each picture below. Print the missing beginning and ending letters to complete each word.

1.  u	2. 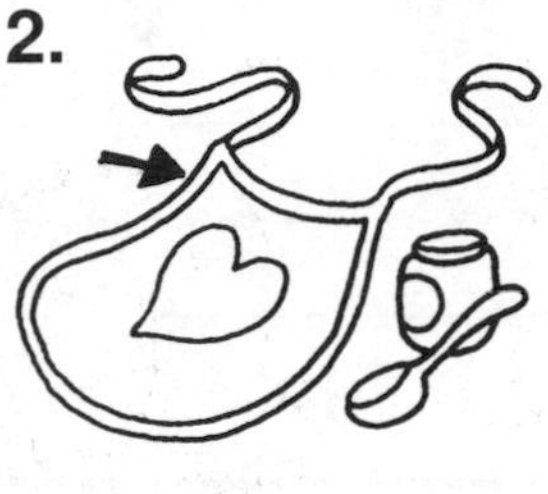 i	3.  a	4.  o
5.  u	6.  u	7. 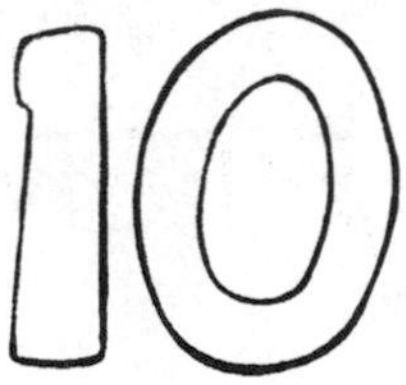 e	8.  o
9.  a	10.  e	11.  i	12.  o
13. 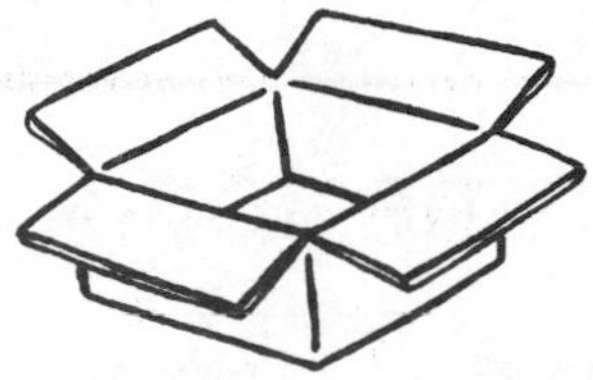 o	14. 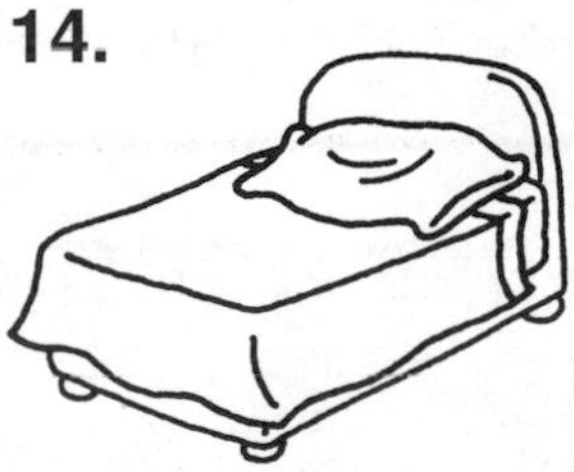 e	15.  i	16.  u

Short Vowel Review

Directions: Circle the correct word that will complete the sentence. Then print the word on the line.

1. Sue had a black _____ .

cat
can't
crate

2. The cat was _____ .

sink
sick
stick

3. She took him to the _____ .

vent
vat
vet

4. He gave the cat a _____ .

shot
shoot
shut

5. Sue gave the cat a _____ .

hug
hut
huge

6. What is a good name for a cat?

_____

Unit Review

Directions: Say the name of each picture. Draw a line to the letter representing its vowel sound.

a

e

i

o

u

Unit Review

Directions: Say the name of each picture. Print the name of the picture on the line.

1. The _____ is fat.

2. The man wears a _____.

3. The _____ is hot.

4. Buster is a _____.

5. The _____ is green.

6. The _____ can swim.

UNIT 3
Long Vowels

Long Aa

Directions: *Cake* has the long sound of **a**. Circle each picture whose name has the long sound of **a**.

Long Aa

Directions: Say the name of each picture. Circle its name.

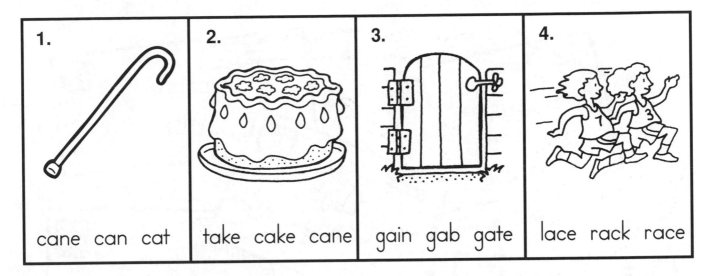

1. cane can cat

2. take cake cane

3. gain gab gate

4. lace rack race

5. hay day date

6. vase van vane

7. bake rake bay

8. face bail base

9. face fail base

10. lay lake late

11. play pay day

12. tap tape tail

Long Aa

Directions: Color each piece of mail that has rhyming long **a** words.

case
lace

cane
can

cage
flag

ran
rain

pain
Zane

dame
flame

sail
jail

nail
pail

tape
tap

take
fake

date
wait

May
say

Long Aa

Directions: Help the train get to the depot. Draw a line from the train to the first word with the long **a** sound. Draw a line to each long **a** word until the train is at the depot!

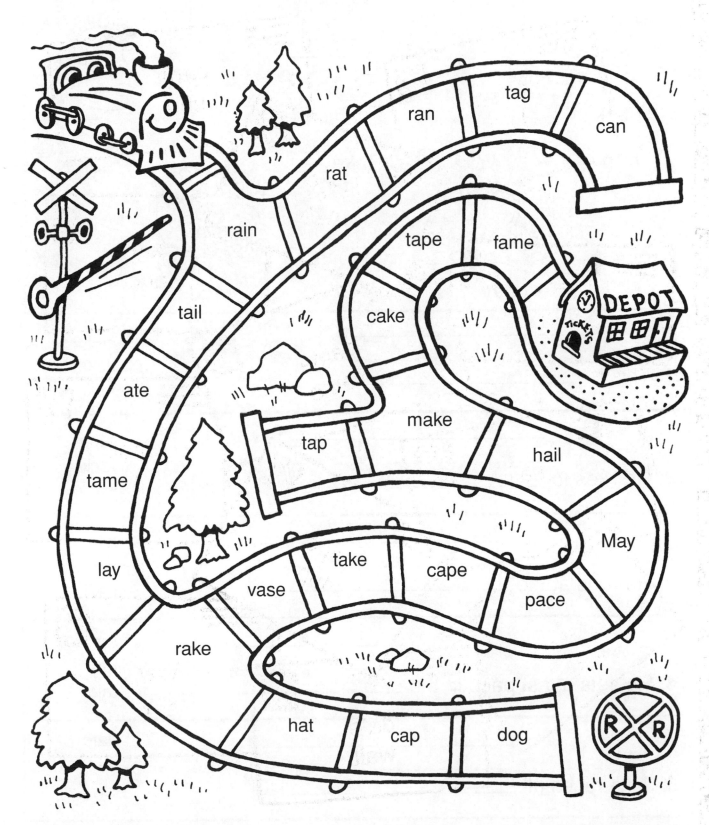

Long Aa

Directions: Look at a sentence. Circle the word that will finish it. Print the word on the line. Use the pictures as clues.

rain

lake

Jake

day

race

1. This is _____ .	Rake Jake Lake
2. He likes to _____ .	race rack ray
3. He runs at the _____ .	late lay lake
4. He sets a fast pace in the _____ .	rat ran rain
5. Jake races all _____ !	date day say

Long Ii

Directions: *Hive* has the long sound of **i**. Circle each picture whose name has the long sound of **i**.

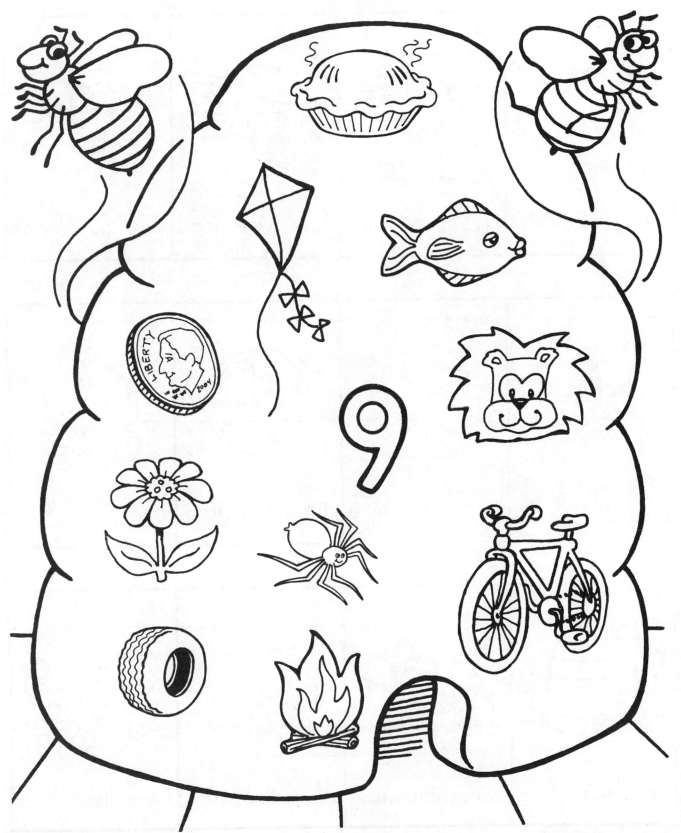

Long Ii

Ii

Directions: Say the name of each picture. Circle its name.

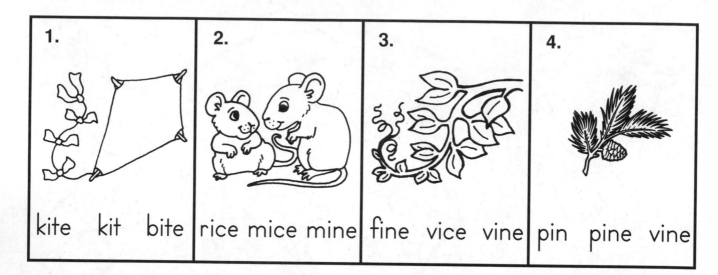

1. kite   kit   bite

2. rice   mice   mine

3. fine   vice   vine

4. pin   pine   vine

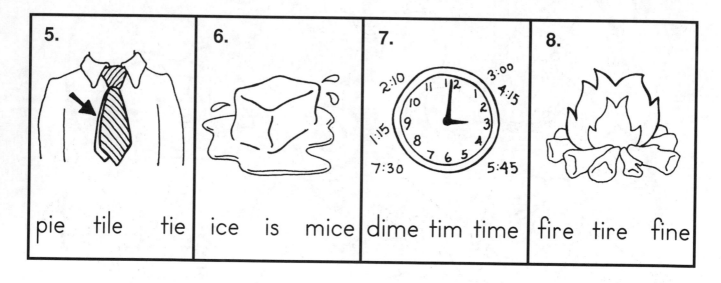

5. pie   tile   tie

6. ice   is   mice

7. dime   tim   time

8. fire   tire   fine

9. hit   hive   five

10. wire   fire   wide

11. dine   dice   mice

12. hive   like   hike

Long Ii

Directions: Color each kite that has rhyming long **i** words.

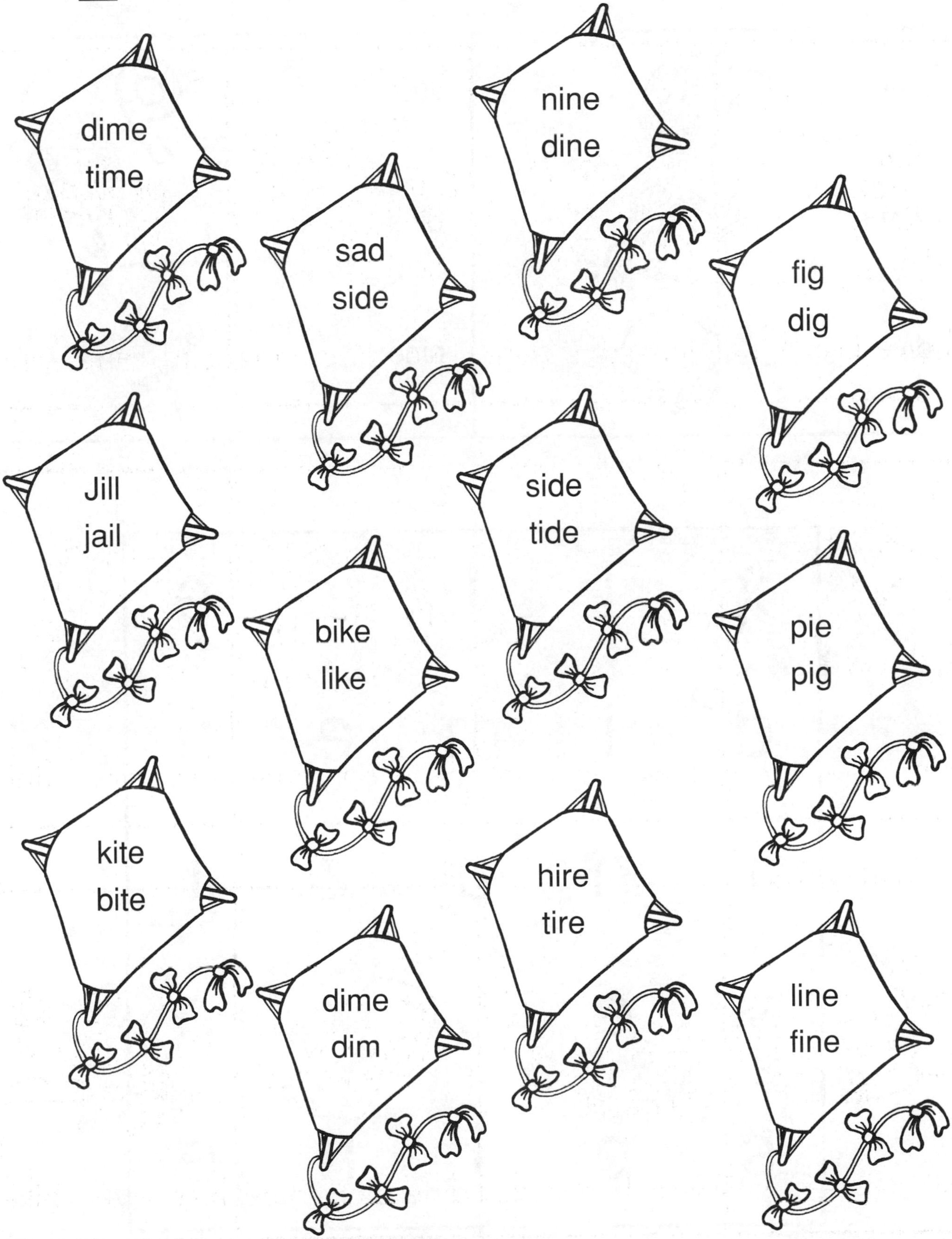

dime
time

nine
dine

sad
side

fig
dig

Jill
jail

side
tide

bike
like

pie
pig

kite
bite

hire
tire

dime
dim

line
fine

Long Ii

Directions: Draw a line from each word to its picture. Then circle the words in the puzzle.

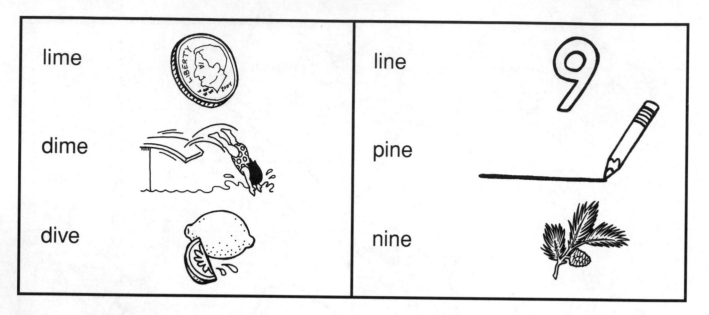

lime	line
dime	pine
dive	nine

```
x  l  i  m  e

d  i  m  e  n

i  n  a  z  i

v  e  b  x  n

e  p  i  n  e
```

Long Ii

I i

Directions: Look at a sentence. Circle the word that will finish it. Print the word on the line. Use the pictures as clues.

1. Mike has a _____.	bite kit kite
2. He thinks it is _____.	fine dine vine
3. It is bigger than _____.	mire mine min
4. He will fly it at _____.	fire five jive
5. He will be on _____.	time tim lime

Long Aa and Ii Review

Directions: Say the name of each picture. If the vowel sound is short **a** or short **i**, circle the word *short*. If the vowel sound is long, circle the word *long*.

1.	2.	3.
short long	short long	short long
4.	5.	6.
short long	short long	short long
7.	8.	9.
short long	short long	short long

Long Uu

Directions: Tube has the long sound of **u**. Circle each picture whose name has the long sound of **u**.

Long Uu

Directions: Say the name of each picture. Circle its name.

1. due   gum   glue

2. tub   tube   lube

3. Luke   Lug   Lid

4. dud   dude   rude

5. cut   cube   cute

6. June   Jam   Jug

7. fruit   fit   suit

8. flat   jute   flute

9. run   ruler   rude

10. dune   duke   duck

11. Dip   Duke   Dud

12. tug   tame   tune

Long Uu

Directions: Circle each piece of fruit that has rhyming long **u** words.

June
dune

fruit
suit

tube
cube

mule
rule

mule
mull

huge
hug

cute
lute

cube
cub

duke
due

true
blue

dude
rude

Luke
Duke

Long Uu

Uu

Directions: Read the words in the list below. Print a word in the puzzle to name each picture.

Across

1    3    5

Down

1    2    4

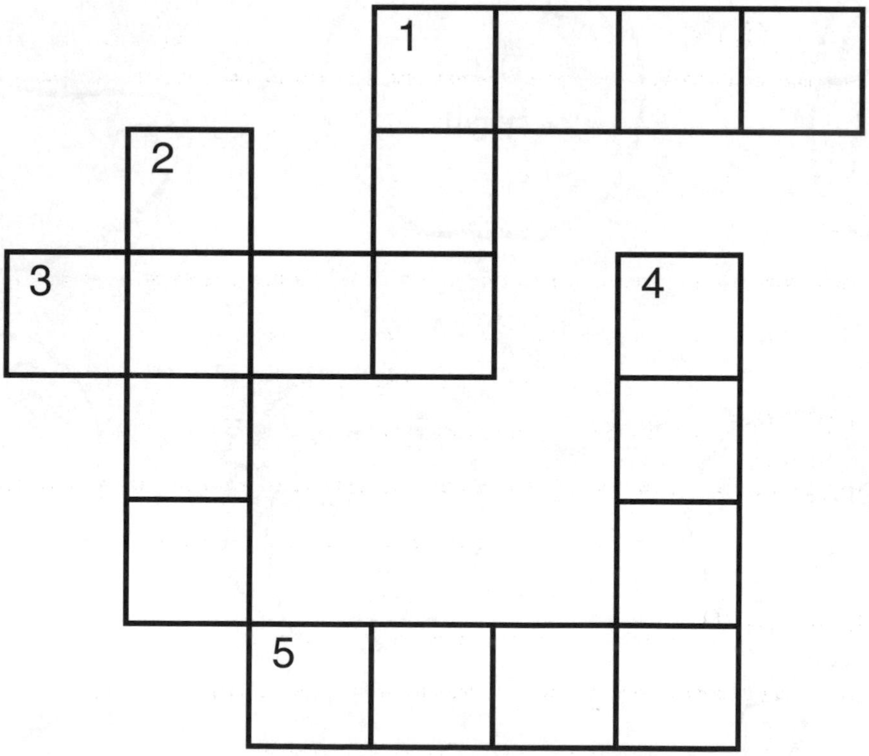

June   Sue   mule   tube   suit   Duke

Long Uu

Directions: Look at a sentence. Circle the word that will finish it. Print the word on the line. Use the pictures as clues.

tune

June

Sue

flute

glue

1. I see _____ .	Sue Due Hue
2. She likes to use _____ .	true clue glue
3. Her birthday is in _____ .	Dune June Tune
4. She got a cute _____ .	jute late flute
5. Now she can play a _____ !	tune rule huge

Long Aa, Ii, and Uu Review

Directions: Circle the words that have the long **a**, long **i**, or long **u** sound.

a	snack ran base at
	snake rain bass ate

i	pine rid ripe fine
	pin ride rip fin

u	tube cute dud jute
	tub cut dude jut

Long Oo

Directions: Follow the objects that contain the long **o** sound to complete the maze.

Long Oo

Directions: Say the name of each picture. If you hear the long **o** sound, color the box labeled *long*. If you hear the short **o** sound, color the box labeled *short*.

1.	2.	3.	4.
short long	short long	short long	short long
5.	**6.**	**7.**	**8.**
short long	short long	short long	short long
9.	**10.**	**11.**	**12.**
short long	short long	short long	short long
13.	**14.**	**15.**	**16.**
short long	short long	short long	short long

Long Oo

Directions: Say the name of each picture. Write the letters for each word.

Long Oo

Directions: Read the sentences below and follow the directions.

1. Draw a goat driving a boat.

2. Draw a bone lying on a stone.

3. Draw a toad sitting on a road.

4. Draw Joan eating a cone.

5. Draw Joe playing in the snow.

6. Draw a nose smelling a rose.

Long Oo

Directions: Use the words in the box below to complete the sentences. Print the rhyming words.

rope	snow	row
note	toe	goat

1. Boat rhymes with _____ .

2. Joe rhymes with _____ .

3. Vote rhymes with _____ .

4. Tow rhymes with _____ .

5. Blow rhymes with _____ .

6. Hope rhymes with _____ .

Long Aa, Ii, Uu, and Oo Review

Directions: Match the long **a**, long **i**, long **u**, and long **o** pictures. Draw a line from a picture to another picture in the box with the same long vowel sound.

Long Ee

E e

Directions: *Sheep* contains the long sound of **e**. Circle each picture that also contains the **e** sound.

Long Ee

 Directions: Say each picture name. Draw a line to the matching word. Then trace the word.

1.

leaf

2.

beans

3.

eat

4.

breathe

5.

jeep

6.

weed

Long Ee

E e **Directions:** Say the name of each picture. Circle the correct word.

1.	**2.**	**3.**
pe pea pae	meat mete meete	sea seal sele
4.	**5.**	**6.**
eat eet ete	hete heat haet	esst easte east
7.	**8.**	**9.**
eel ele eele	tre treet tree	sea seea ese
10.	**11.**	**12.**
be bea bee	three tree there	foot fete feet

Long Ee

Ee

Directions: Say the name of each picture. Print the correct letter(s) in the spaces below to provide the missing long **e** sound in each word.

1.	2.
b___	s___ d

3.	4.
f___t	___agle

5.	6.
sl___p	cr___am

7.	8.
wh___l	wr___ath

9.	10.
h___l	mu___

Long Ee

Directions: Say the name of each picture. Color the boxes that contain a word that rhymes with the name of the picture.

bee

three	trick	tree	trim	treat
free	week	wine	me	wee

weed

tweed	bread	bead	bean	went
wed	wheel	seed	heed	need

meat

mate	met	feat	mite	heat
Pete	bite	beet	bate	beat

peek

sneak	take	rake	wake	emu
freak	snake	lake	meek	reek

Long Vowel Review

Directions: Say the name of each picture. Circle the letter that makes the long vowel sound within each word.

1. a e i o u	**2.** a e i o u	**3.** a e i o u
4. a e i o u	**5.** a e i o u	**6.** a e i o u
7. a e i o u	**8.** a e i o u	**9.** a e i o u
10. a e i o u	**11.** a e i o u	**12.** a e i o u
13. a e i o u	**14.** a e i o u	**15.** a e i o u

Long Vowel Review

Directions: Blend the sounds together to say each word. Circle the correct picture.

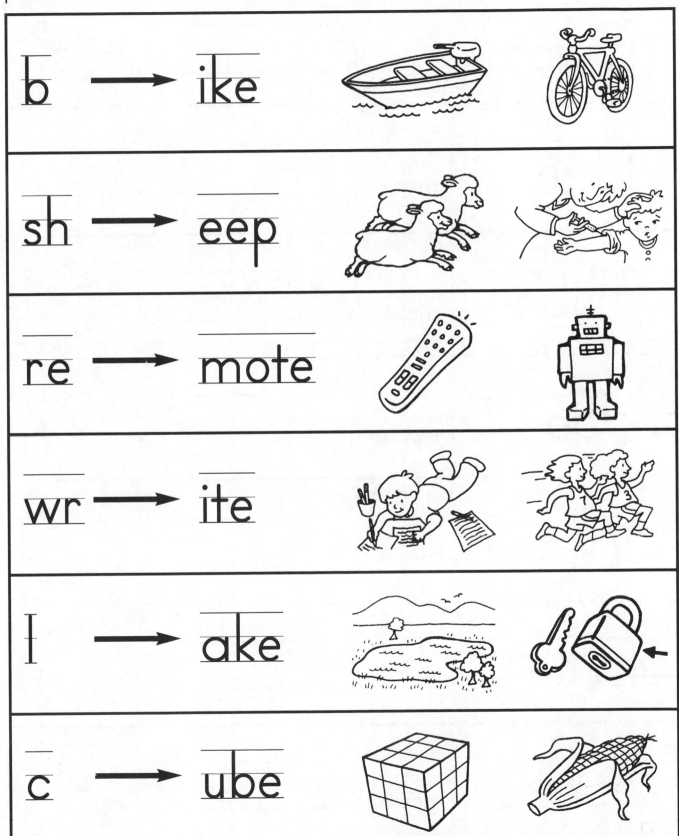

Long Vowel Review

Directions: Read the word on the left, and write the rhyming word to its right.

1. Goat   rhymes with _____ .

2. Bite   rhymes with _____ .

3. Tube   rhymes with _____ .

4. Joe   rhymes with _____ .

5. Wake   rhymes with _____ .

6. Free   rhymes with _____ .

7. Shake   rhymes with _____ .

Unit Review

Directions: Say the name of each picture. Fill in the bubble beside its long vowel sound.

1.
○ a
○ e
○ i
○ o
○ u

2.
○ a
○ e
○ i
○ o
○ u

3.
○ a
○ e
○ i
○ o
○ u

4.
○ a
○ e
○ i
○ o
○ u

5.
○ a
○ e
○ i
○ o
○ u

6.
○ a
○ e
○ i
○ o
○ u

7.
○ a
○ e
○ i
○ o
○ u

8.
○ a
○ e
○ i
○ o
○ u

Unit Review

Directions: Say the name of each picture. Unscramble the letters to print the name of the picture on each line.

1.  epesh

2.  esragp

3.  keit

4.  elum

5.  oagt

6.  caret

7.  eeb

8.  aet

UNIT 4
Consonant Blends and Y as a Vowel

R Blends

Directions: Choose two colors to use for each present. Use the same color for the parts of the present that begin with the same beginning blend.

1.

2.

3.

4.

R Blends

Directions: Say the name of each picture. Circle its name.

1. cry try	**2.** tuck truck	**3.** grape grin
4. track truck	**5.** prince pin	**6.** fruit suit
7. crib crab	**8.** grin grapes	**9.** train track
10. brush rush	**11.** crane crab	**12.** drill drop

R Blends

Directions: Name each picture. Write the letters for the beginning blend on the line. Then trace the whole word.

1. oceries

2. esent

3. iangle

4. idge

5. incess

6. agon

7. ame

8. ide

R Blends

Directions: Say the name of each picture. Find a row with three pictures beginning with the same blend. Draw a line through the three pictures and write the beginning blend on the line.

1.

_____

_____

2.

L Blends

Directions: Circle the three pictures in each row that have the same beginning blend.

L Blends

Directions: Read each word. If it begins with a blend, color the petal.

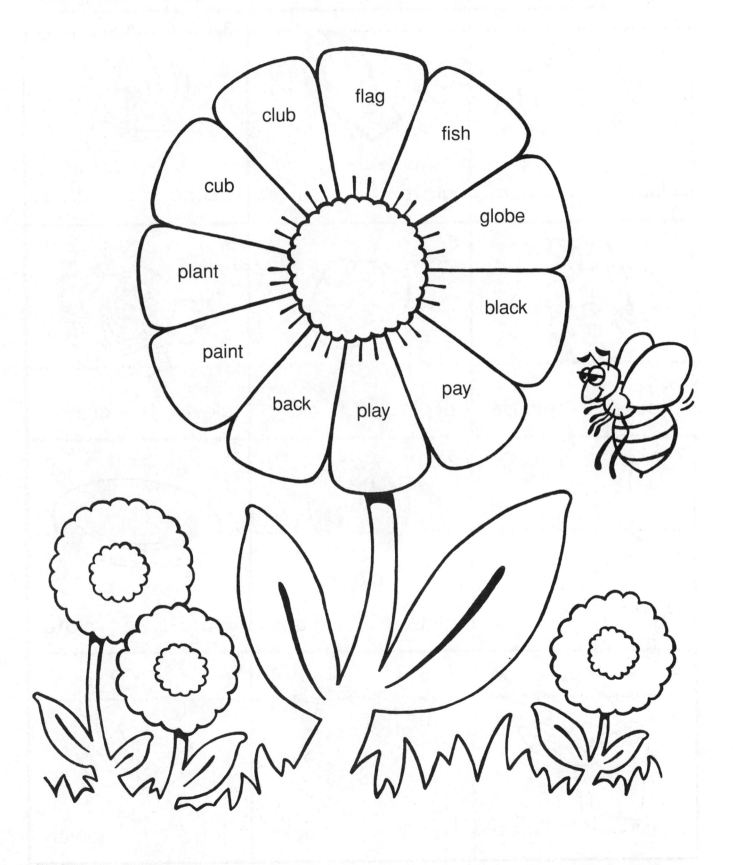

L Blends

Directions: Say the name of each picture. Circle its name.

1. plug plum	**2.** glove love	**3.** flame flop
4. mouse blouse	**5.** clip clam	**6.** clown crown
7. flat flute	**8.** globe robe	**9.** plant plate
10. class clap	**11.** blocks locks	**12.** flag flower

L Blends

Directions: Name the picture. Write its beginning blend. Then trace the whole word.

1.  _ _ edge

2.  _ _ anket

3.  _ _ iers

4.  _ _ arinet

5.  _ _ ashlight

6.  _ _ amingo

S Blends

Directions: Say the name of each picture in the first column. Circle each picture in the row that begins with the same blend as the first picture.

S Blends

Directions: Say the name of each picture. Circle the correct word that spells its name.

1. ski sing	2. net nest	3. sled send
4. slide slow	5. stamp stomp	6. spoke smoke
7. sway swing	8. star stone	9. stamp stump
10. swing swim	11. sponge spank	12. spaghetti spray

S Blends

Directions: Say the name of each picture. Print the correct letter in each box to complete the s-blend words.

S Blends

Directions: Say the name of each picture. Find and circle the matching word in the puzzle below.

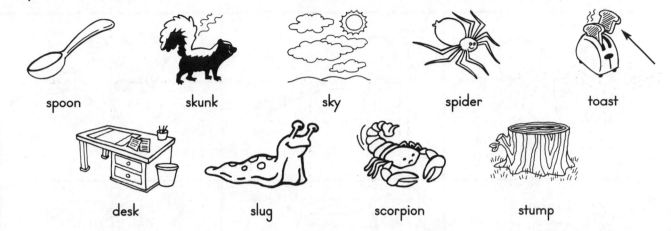

spoon   skunk   sky   spider   toast

desk   slug   scorpion   stump

```
s p i d e r s s
s s s e s s k s
t o a s t k u p
s s s k u y n o
s l u g m s k o
s c o r p i o n
```

Final Blends

Directions: Say the name of each picture. Circle the blend found at the end of each word.

1. sk mp	2. sk mp	3. sk mp
4. sk mp	5. sk mp	6. sk mp
7. sk mp	8. sk mp	9. sk mp
10. sk mp	11. sk mp	12. sk mp
13. sk mp	14. sk mp	15. sk mp

Final Blends

Directions: Write a story using at least five of the final consonant blend words below. Then illustrate the story.

| pump | jump | lamp | disk | stomp | blimp |
| bump | desk | champ | chimp | mask | task |

_____

- -

_____

- -

_____

- -

_____

- -

_____

- -

_____

- -

_____

My Illustration

Final Blends

Directions: Name each picture. Circle the two pictures in each circle that end with the same blend.

1.
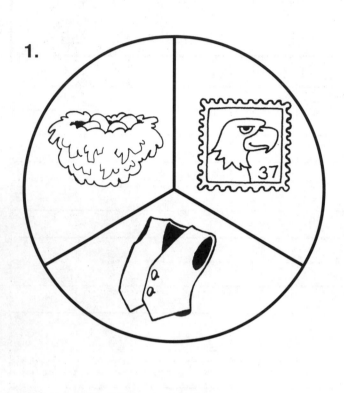

2.
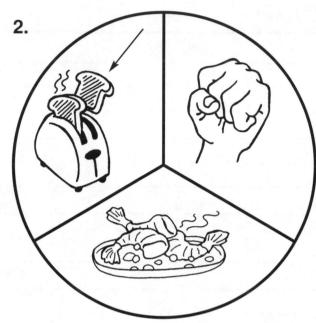

3.

4.

Final Blends

Directions: Say the name of each picture. Circle its name.

1.	2.	3.
west nest	bank tank	list fist
4.	5.	6.
most coast	junk bunk	mink rink
7.	8.	9.
wink mink	wink sink	west vest
10.	11.	12.
rink think	fast mast	west vest

Final Blends

Directions: Blend the letter sounds as you say each word. Then color the picture it names.

1. w ⟶ ing	(ring)	(wing)
2. s ⟶ ing	(singer)	(bee with stinger)
3. r ⟶ ing	(swing)	(ring)
4. k ⟶ ing	(wing)	(king)
5. sw ⟶ ing	(singer)	(swing)

Final Blends

Directions: Look at the picture in each box. Circle the word that matches the picture. Print the word on the line.

1.	king kong	_____
2.	sing spring	_____
3.	rang ring	_____
4.	swing swan	_____
5.	spring sing	_____
6.	string spring	_____
7.	sing sting	_____

Y as a Vowel

Directions: Say the name of each picture. Print the missing letter. Then trace the whole word.

1.	**2.**	**3.**	**4.**
lad___	pla___	pra___	spra___
5.	**6.**	**7.**	**8.**
fair___	Ma___	penn___	b___e
9.	**10.**	**11.**	**12.**
bugg___	pon___	sk___	sp___

Y as a Vowel

Directions: Unscramble each word. Then write the word on the line next to it, using **y** as a vowel.

1.	ysp	_____
2.	syk	_____
3.	yrc	_____
4.	fyr	_____
5.	yluJ	_____
6.	lfy	_____
7.	ypon	_____

Y as a Vowel

Directions: Say the name of each picture. Circle the words in the boxes that have the same **y** as a vowel sound.

candy

| handy | yam | Mandy | year | yet |
| yo-yo | yuck | dandy | yoke | yarn |

spy

| cyst | fly | my | bean | spry |
| by | buy | cry | try | bye |

sky

| fry | pry | retry | ply | why |
| year | try | play | hay | fray |

lady

| baby | tray | penny | wake | cry |
| yarn | yes | buggy | lazy | ray |

Y as a Vowel

Directions: Say the name of each picture. Write the correct word in the space provided to finish the sentence.

pony	cry	fly	July

1. The baby started to _____.

2. She swatted a _____.

3. The girl loved her _____.

4. It was the 4th of _____.

Blends Review

Directions: Say the name of each picture in the first column. Circle each picture whose name ends with the same blend within the row.

king

bump

test

flask

wink

Blends Review

Directions: Name each picture. Write its name in the crossword puzzle next to it. Use the words in the box.

plus	fly	snow	flag	fries
bride	plug	frog	snake	broom

Blends Review

Directions: Say the name of each picture. Draw a line to the letters that represent its blend sound.

Blends Review

Directions: Draw a line from the star to the next picture with a beginning blend. Draw a line to each beginning blend picture until you reach the stop sign.

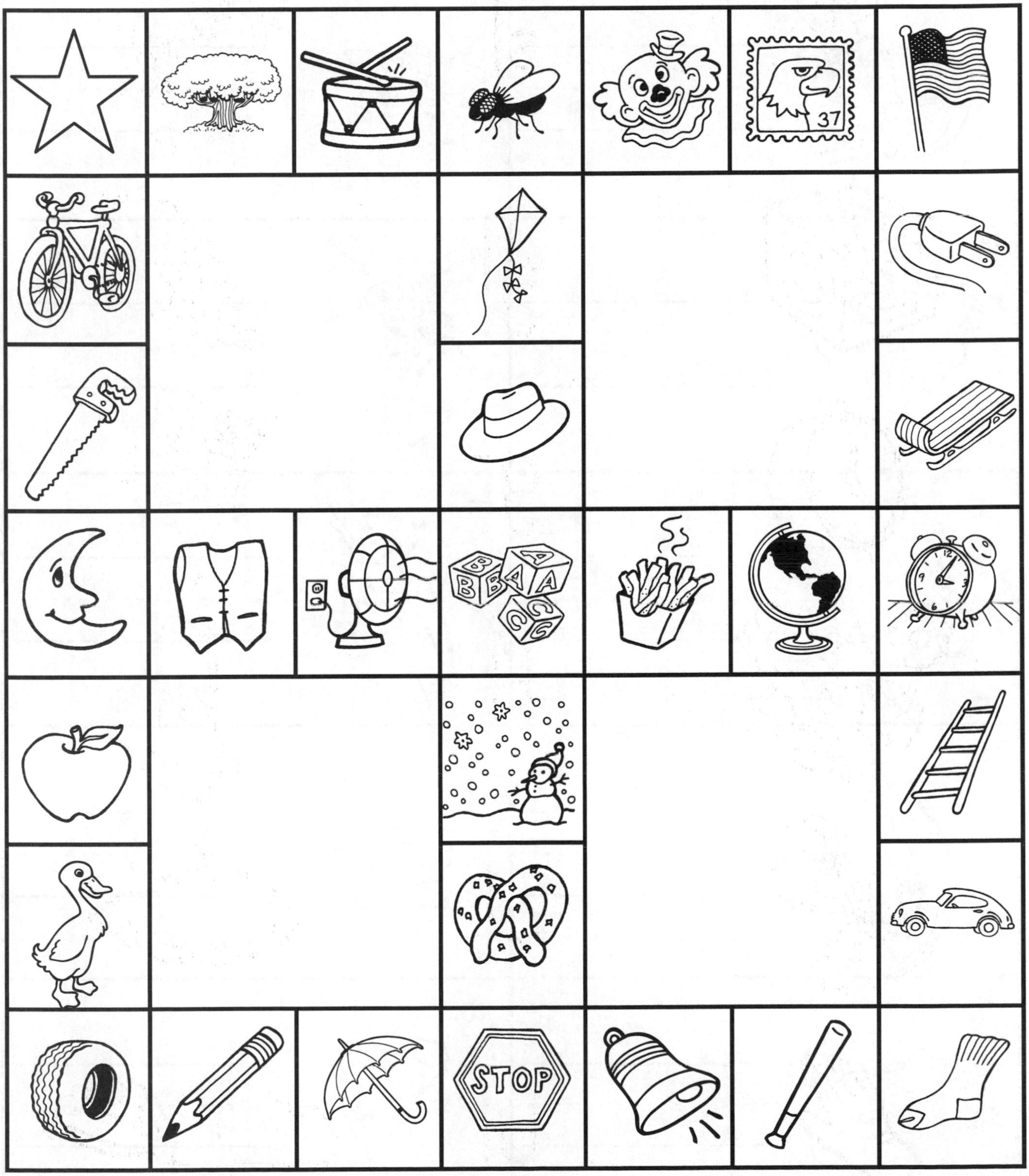

Blends Review

Directions: Say the name of each picture. Print its ending blend on the line and then trace the whole word.

1. si _____

2. ma _____

3. ne _____

4. toa _____

5. mi _____

6. ju _____

7. ve _____

8. che _____

9. de _____

10. fi _____

Blends Review

Directions: Read each word below. Print the words in the correct column representing its blend.

best	milk	glove	plow	glow
plane	vest	silk	gland	bilk
play	please	sulk	story	bulk

st	pl	gl	lk

Blends and Y Review

Directions: Read the sentences. Use the mixed-up letters to make a word. Print the word on the line to finish the sentence.

1. Fran is _____ friend. | ym

2. Today she will _____ Stan. | amryr

3. I see a gold _____. | nowcr

4. The _____ is the best man! | ikgn

5. Look at the _____. | cclko

6. It is time to _____! | atrst

Unit Review

Directions: Circle the blend that begins the word. Write the word on the line.

1. fl fr	2. sp st	3. br bl
_____ ag	_____ oon	_____ aid

4. gl fl	5. Fl Fr	6. sp sm
_____ obe	_____ orida	_____ ill

7. cr cl	8. sp sl	9. pr pl
_____ iff	_____ ider	_____ ane

Unit Review

Directions: Say the name of each picture. Circle its name.

1. dress   desk   dry

2. dry   try   cry

3. swim   swing   swap

4. plug   plum   plant

5. bunny   baby   by

6. slide   bread   sled

7. trunk   bunk   dunk

8. skate   skip   slate

9. grass   glum   glass

10. fair   dairy   fairy

11. wing   king   ring

12. tree   free   tram

UNIT 5
Endings, Digraphs, and Contractions

Inflectional Endings (–ed)

Directions: Read the word beside each picture. Trace the word and then circle the base in each word.

1. floated

2. melted

3. robbed

4. glued

5. mailed

6. shaved

Inflectional Endings (–ing)

ing

Directions: Read the words beside each picture. Trace the word and then circle the base in each word.

1. playing

2. walking

3. swimming

4. running

5. cooking

6. singing

Inflectional Endings (–ed, –ing)

Directions: Print each word below using the **ed** or **ing** endings.

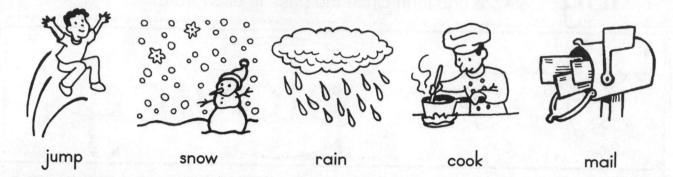

jump   snow   rain   cook   mail

-ed	-ing

Inflectional Endings (–ed, –ing)

Directions: Circle the word that will complete the sentence and then print it on the line.

1.

I was _____ out the window.

looking

looked

2.

I _____ it up.

opening

opened

3.

The dog _____ in a doghouse.

living

lived

4.

My dad _____ French.

studying

studied

5.

I was _____ outside.

playing

played

6.

My mom was _____ dinner.

cooking

cooked

Consonant Digraph (th)

th

Directions: Say the name of each picture. Color the sections that have pictures with the beginning sound of **th**.

Consonant Digraph (wh)

Directions: *Wheel* begins with the sound of **wh**. Color the wheel section if the picture in it begins with the sound of **wh**.

Consonant Digraphs (th, wh)

Directions: Circle each word in the puzzle. Use the pictures as clues.

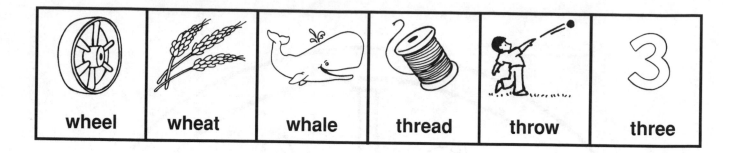

| wheel | wheat | whale | thread | throw | three |

```
q  a  w  h  a  l  e  x
x  t  h  r  e  a  d  w
w  h  e  e  l  x  u
u  r  a  s  p  k  c
d  o  t  h  r  e  e
i  w  m  w  b  x  j
```

Consonant Digraphs (th, wh)

Directions: Circle the word that names the picture. Write the word on the line.

1. when

   wheel

2. thorn

   throw

3. wheel

   whale

4. thud

   think

5. whistle

   wheat

6. thank

   thimble

Consonant Digraph (sh)

Directions: Say the name of each picture. Circle its name.

1.	shark / short / wash
2.	shark / short / wash
3.	sharp / shower / shingle
4.	wash / dish / shot
5.	shut / shuttle / shed
6.	fish / ship / flash
7.	shop / shot / ship
8.	shout / shade / shim
9.	flash / sheep / sheet
10.	show / shop / shower

Consonant Digraph (sh)

sh

Directions: Name each picture below. Print the missing letters to complete each word.

1. __ip	2. __adow	3. __ell	4. __eep
5. __irt	6. __oe	7. __ore	8. __ake
9. bu__	10. __out	11. __ed	12. __elf
13. __ave	14. fi__	15. __ark	16. wa__

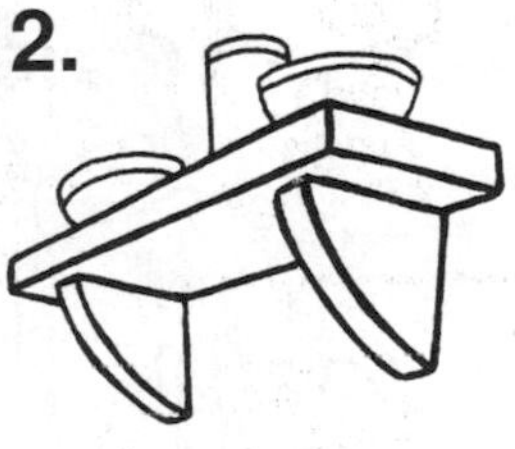

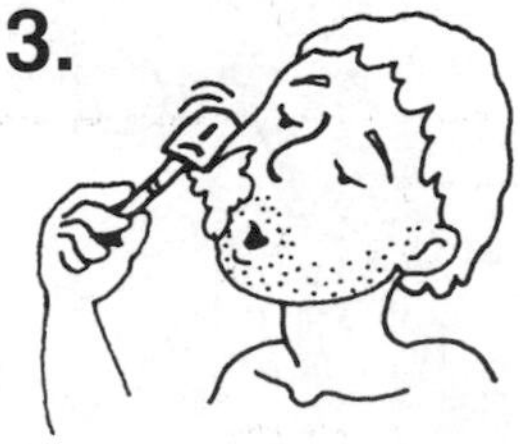

Consonant Digraph (ch)

Directions: Name each picture below. Print the missing letters to complete each word.

1. _____ imp	2. _____ erries	3. _____ eeks
4. _____ ain	5. _____ eese	6. _____ in
7. _____ air	8. _____ ocolate	9. _____ eck
10. _____ alk	11. _____ ick	12. _____ ur

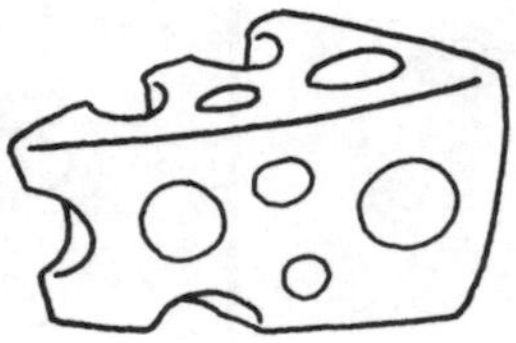

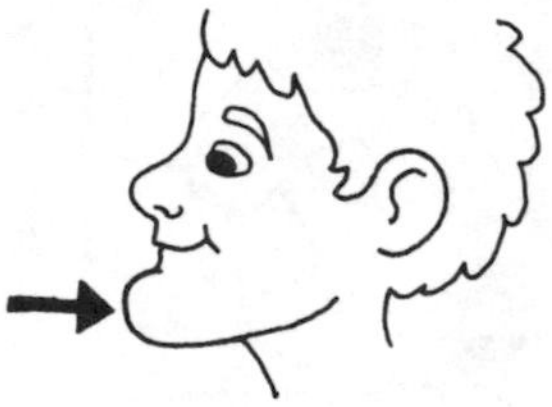

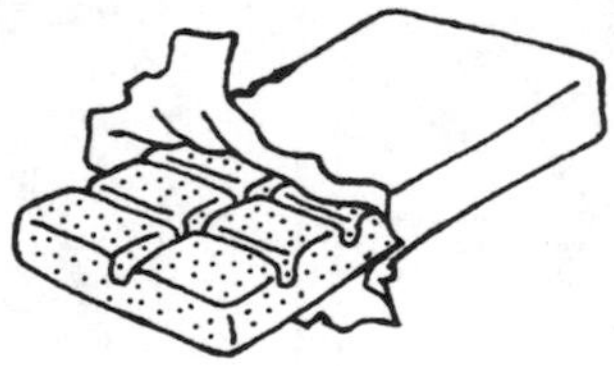

Consonant Digraph (ch)

Directions: Choose from the words in the word bank below to complete the sentences.

chicken   cheese   lunch   chair   cherries

1. Sue is ready for _____ .

2. She has a slice of _____ .

3. She has a piece of _____ .

4. She has some red _____ .

5. Time to sit on a _____ and eat!

Consonant Digraph (kn)

Directions: The letters **kn** make the sound of **n**. Say the name of each picture below and then circle the letters that are making the sound of **n**. Then trace the whole word.

1. 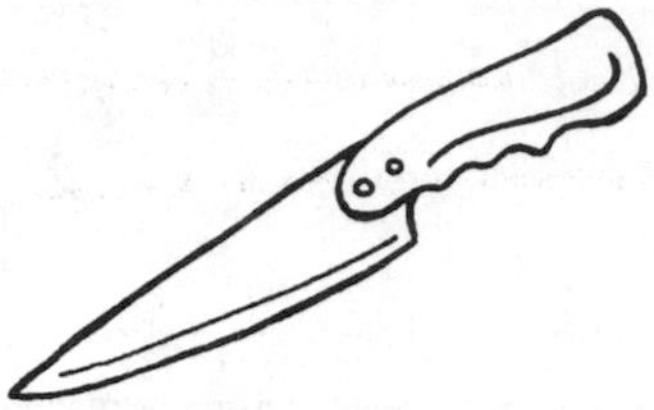 (kn)ife

2.  knight

3.  nurse

4. 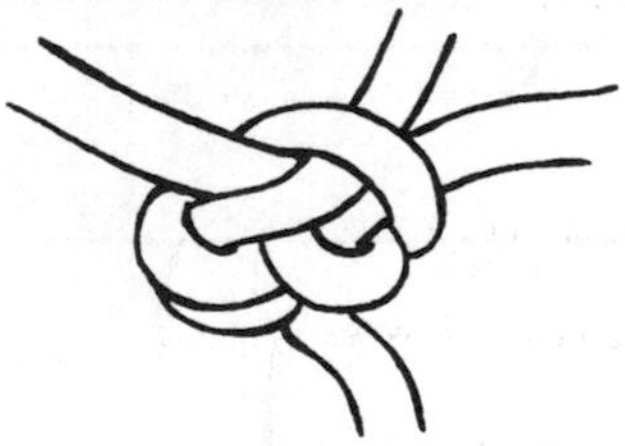 knot

5. 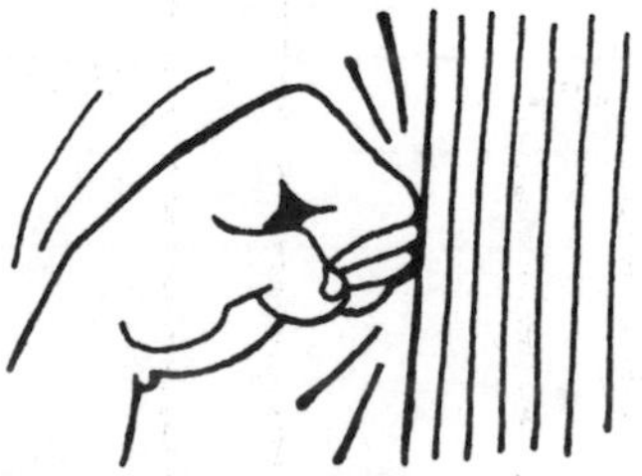 knock

6.  nest

Consonant Digraph (kn)

Directions: The letters **kn** make the sound of **n**. Read each word below and then follow the path of **kn** words to complete the path.

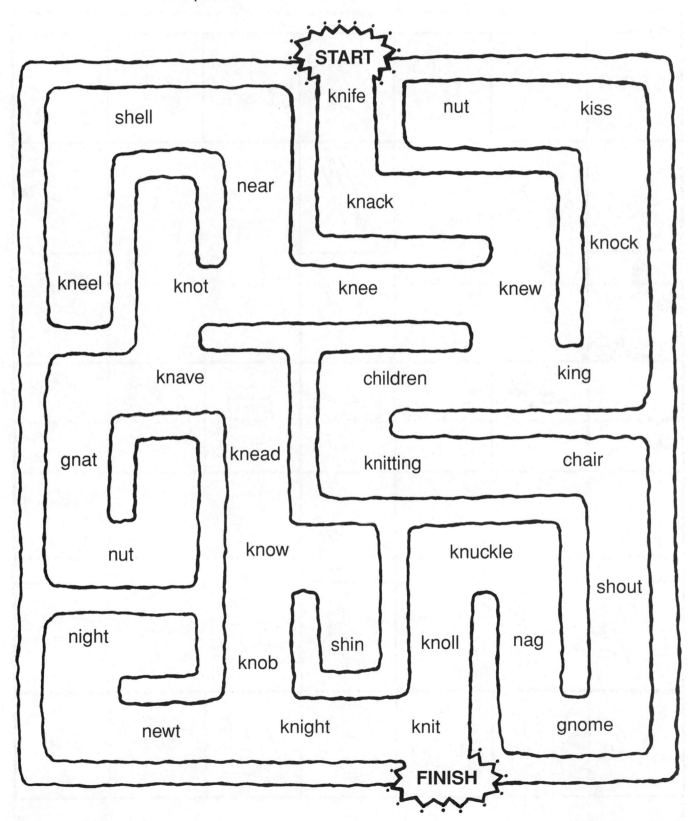

Digraph Review

Directions: Find the pictures with the beginning digraphs **sh**, **wh**, **ch**, and **th**. Draw a line from the word BEGIN to a picture with a beginning digraph. Then draw a line to each beginning digraph picture until you read the word END.

BEGIN					
					END

Digraph Review

Directions: Say the name of each picture in the first column. Circle each picture in the row that contains the same consonant digraph.

Digraph Review

Directions: Read each word below. Print the each word in the correct column representing its blend.

path	chick	shout	what	thing
thread	math	push	gush	chin
chart	short	tooth	shelf	whale

sh	ch	wh	th

Digraph Review

Directions: Complete the crossword puzzle by choosing the correct word from the word box below to complete the sentence.

chess	shoes	thief
whistle	gnaw	knife

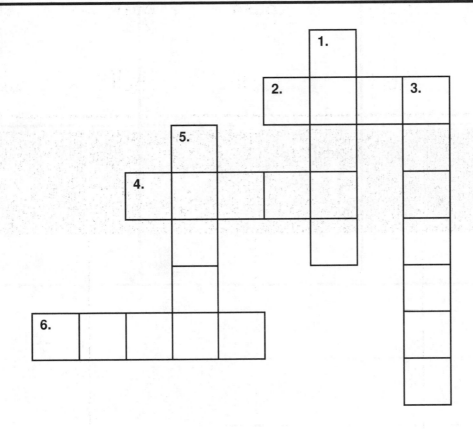

1. A _____ is used to spread butter on toast.

2. Beavers like to _____ on wood.

3. A coach blows a _____ to stop play.

4. A _____ stole all of her money.

5. Sue's _____ have a fancy buckle.

6. Bob loves to play the game of _____.

Digraph Review

Directions: Read the word in each box below. Draw a matching picture in the space on the word bank. Then print the words on the correct line below to complete the sentence.

WORD BANK

sheep	teeth	chair
knot	whistle	chick

1. The _____ has soft wool.

2. A _____ is twisted rope.

3. My _____ are used for chewing.

4. A _____ is blown at noon.

5. I like to sit on a _____ .

6. A _____ hatches from an egg.

Digraphs and Endings Review

Directions: Look at the letters in the first box of each row. Circle the words that have the same beginning or ending letters.

th	throat	throne	time	thug
	thing	tock	thank	tank
ch	chain	crunch	cherry	cat
	cliff	chair	chocolate	cookie
wh	water	whittle	wick	whack
	why	will	wow	whine
-ed	played	playing	sat	stored
	walk	walked	fished	danced
-ing	jumped	jumping	rowing	climb
	chasing	running	drag	drink

Digraphs and Endings Review

Directions: Use the words below to write a story. Then illustrate it.

chair	ship	shore	shell
whale	what	sailing	played
cheese	knife	knot	waved

_____

- -

_____

- -

_____

- -

_____

- -

_____

- -

_____

My Illustration

Contractions

Directions: A contraction is a short way to say and write words. Color each balloon that has a contraction on it.

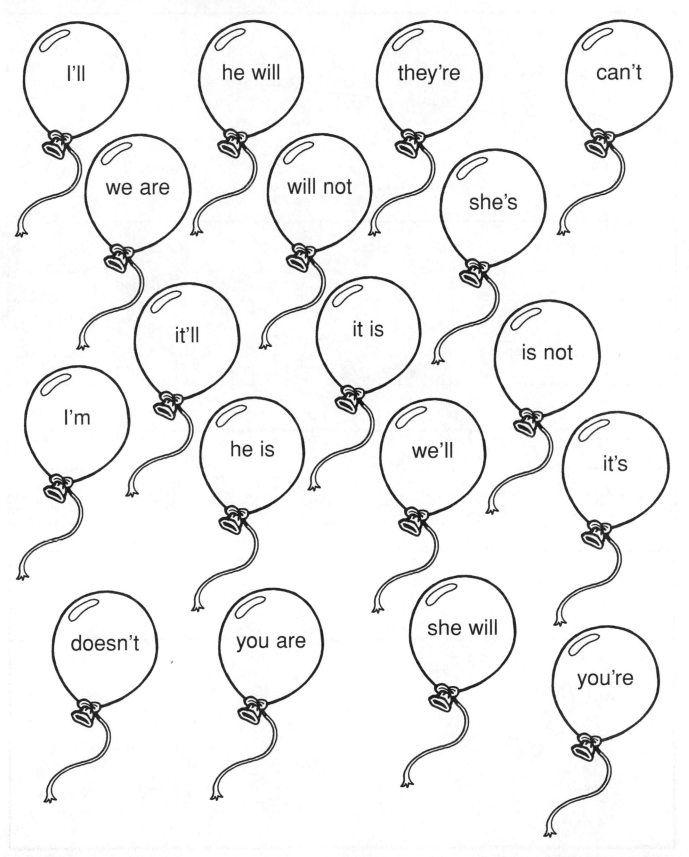

Contractions

Directions: A contraction is a short way to say and write words. Match the contraction and its meaning.

she's	he is
he's	it is
it's	she is

I'll	you will
you'll	I will
he'll	he will

can't	will not
won't	does not
doesn't	cannot

we're	they are
I'm	we are
they're	I am

Contractions

Directions: *She's* is a short way to say "she is." Circle the short way to write the underlined words. Use the words in the box to help you.

she is = she's	he is = he's	it is = it's

1.	<u>It is</u> a sunny day.	It'll It's
2.	<u>He is</u> playing in the sand.	He's She's
3.	<u>She is</u> swimming.	He's She's
4.	<u>It is</u> a fun day at the beach!	It's I'm

Contractions

Directions: *I'm* is a short way to say "I am." Circle the short way to write the underlined words. Use the words in the box to help you.

I am = I'm	we are = we're
you are = you're	they are = they're

1.	<u>I am</u> taking a trip.	I'll I'm
2.	<u>You are</u> coming with me.	You're We're
3.	<u>They are</u> waiting for us.	We're They're
4.	<u>We are</u> going to the mountains.	We're You're

Contractions

Directions: *Isn't* is a short way to say "is not." Circle the short way to write the underlined words. Use the words in the box to help you.

cannot = can't	is not = isn't
will not = won't	does not = doesn't

1.	I <u>cannot</u> find my ticket.	can't isn't
2.	It <u>is not</u> in my bag.	can't isn't
3.	The show <u>does not</u> start yet.	won't doesn't
4.	We <u>will not</u> miss it!	won't doesn't

Contractions

Directions: *I'll* is a short way to say "I will." Circle the short way to write the underlined words. Use the words in the box to help you.

I will = I'll	he will = he'll	she will = she'll
we will = we'll	you will = you'll	it will = it'll

1. <u>I will</u> bring the sandwiches.
   I'll
   I'm

2. <u>He will</u> bring the chips.
   She'll
   He'll

3. <u>She will</u> bring the cookies.
   He'll
   She'll

4. <u>You will</u> bring the plates.
   You'll
   You're

5. <u>We will</u> have a picnic.
   You'll
   We'll

6. <u>It will</u> be fun!
   It's
   It'll

Contractions

Directions: Help the car get to its garage. Draw a line from the car to the first contraction. Draw a line to each contraction until you reach the right house.

can't

doesn't

I'll

they're

I

it's

do not   I can

don't

I will

it is

isn't

he will

it's   you're

she is

he'll

won't   she's

they are   I am   will not   she will   he is

is not   we are

Contractions and Endings Review

Directions: Read the words. Make lists by writing each word in its correct column.

jumping	talked	isn't	raked
painted	you're	playing	singing
it'll	dancing	rained	she'll
sinking	we'll	hunted	reading
skated	he's		

−ing words	−ed words	contractions

Unit Review

Directions: Say the name of each picture. Circle its name.

1. 30 thin thirty three	**2.** wheat white why	**3.** knot knob knee
4. chin chips chain	**5.** sheep ship sheet	**6.** thick thank think
7. knit knife knock	**8.** chip chair cherry	**9.** whip white while
10. knot knob knock	**11.** chum church chill	**12.** throne thorn tie

Unit Review

Directions: Underline the sentence that tells about the picture.

1.		We're taking a walk. We're eating candy. It's raining today.
2.		The bunny hopped away. The bunny skated on the pond. He jumped on the tramp.
3.		I can't find my kitty. He's jumping on the tramp. The clothes are drying.
4.		We're making popcorn. She's baking a cake. They're riding bikes.
5.		He's riding a trike. He's jogging on the track. He's riding a horse.
6.		He tugged on the rope. He can't find his hat. She won't pet the dog.

Answer Key

Answer Key

Page 5
Color stars with the following letters: Tt, Rr, Ll, Ss, Gg, Dd, Ff, Bb, hH, nN, Mm, Jj, kK.

Page 6
Color the following pictures: 7, Santa, sink, sock, saw, sandwich.

Page 7
Color the turtles that include the following pictures: turkey, television, tiger, top, toothbrush, tent, tire.

Page 8
Circle the following pictures: bike, bird, bell, bow, book, bed, bananas, box, bat, bear.

Page 9
1. Bb	5. Ss	9. Tt
2. Bb	6. Tt	10. Ss
3. Tt	7. Bb	11. Ss
4. Bb	8. Ss	12. Tt

Page 10
Color the following pictures: hat, heart, hose, horn, hay, hotdog, ham, hammer.

Page 11
Circle the following pictures: mountains, marshmallows, monkey, mouse, moon, money, mailbox, man.

Page 12
Circle the following pictures: key, kitchen, king, koala, kitten, kangaroo.

Page 13
1. Hh	5. Hh	9. Hh
2. Mm	6. Mm	10. Mm
3. Kk	7. Kk	11. Hh
4. Kk	8. Mm	12. Kk

Page 14
Check to make sure two pictures start with the j sound.

Page 15
Color the following pictures: fire, fish, feet, fork, fan, 5, flower.

Page 16
Circle the following pictures: gas, gorilla, guitar, gum, girl, goat, game.

Page 17
1. Ff	5. Gg	9. Jj
2. Gg	6. Jj	10. Ff
3. Jj	7. Gg	11. Ff
4. Ff	8. Ff	12. Jj

Page 18
Circle the following pictures: lion, lemonade, ladder, ladybug, lamp, lollipop.

Page 19
Color the doors with the following pictures: duck, desk, donkey, dinosaur, dog, donuts, drum, deer.

Page 20
Color the notes with the following pictures: nest, newspaper, nail, net, necklace, nickel, nose, 9.

Page 21
1. Ll	5. Ll	9. Nn
2. Dd	6. Ll	10. Dd
3. Nn	7. Dd	11. Ll
4. Nn	8. Nn	12. Dd

Page 22
Color the magnifying glasses with the following letters: rR, Ww, cC, vV, Xx, Rr, qQ, Pp, zZ, Qq, Yy.

Page 23
Circle the following pictures: worm, well, watch, wagon, windmill, walrus, wallet, web.

Page 24
Color the scoops that have the following pictures: cat, carrots, candle, cake, corn, cup.

Page 25
Circle the following pictures inside the ring: robot, rabbit, rainbow, rocket, rake, rose.

Page 26
1. Ww	5. Cc	9. Rr
2. Cc	6. Rr	10. Ww
3. Rr	7. Ww	11. Cc
4. Ww	8. Cc	12. Rr

Page 27
Circle the following pictures inside the pumpkin: pillow, pan, puppy, pencil, penny, pot, pants, pig, purse, popcorn.

Page 28
Color the squares that have the following pictures: queen, quarter, quail, quiet, quill, question.

Page 29
Circle the following pictures inside the valentine: vegetables, van, vest, vacuum, vase, volcano.

Page 30
1. Pp	5. Pp	9. Pp
2. Qq	6. Qq	10. Qq
3. Vv	7. Vv	11. Vv
4. Vv	8. Qq	12. Pp

Page 31
Circle the following pictures: fox, box, ax, sax. The letter x should be filled in all blanks at the bottom of the page.

Page 32
Circle the following pictures inside the yak: yarn, yo-yo, yawn. The letter y should be filled in all blanks at the bottom of the page.

Page 33
Circle the following pictures inside the zoo: zucchini, zigzag, zebra, zipper, 0. The letter z should be filled in all blanks at the bottom of the page.

Page 34
1. s	5. m	9. n	13. f
2. t	6. x	10. k	14. d
3. b	7. d	11. g	15. g
4. t	8. m	12. t	16. p or g

Page 35
The words are as follows: six, rug, four, jeep, run, fin, sun, pen. The secret message is "surprise."

Page 36
The lines should be draw from the following pictures to the correct letters: giraffe–r, apple–p, ruler–l, seven–v, donut–n, spider–d, wagon–g, vacuum–c

Page 37
1. b	4. d	7. l
2. t	5. v	8. g
3. p	6. b	9. g

Page 38
1. middle l		7. last n
2. last t		8. first b
3. first m		9. middle v
4. last p		10. last f
5. last x		11. middle d
6. first c		12. first y

Page 39
1. c, p or m, g		7. b, t
2. g, m		8. w, b
3. h, t		9. r, g
4. f, n		10. w, g
5. s, n		11. z, p
6. j, t		12. s, x

Page 41
Color the following signs: aA, Uu, Ii, Oo, and eE.

Page 42
Circle the following pictures: ant, candy, bat, rabbit, map, candle, and lamp.

Page 43
1. ant	5. mat	9. bag
2. lad	6. bat	10. pants
3. tack	7. crab	11. pan
4. map	8. sand	12. hat

Page 44
Color the following pictures: pan, ram, cat, dad, and tag.

Page 45
The path should be as follows: cat, fan, ant, fad, rack, at, lamp, and, map.

Page 46
1. van	4. tag
2. dad	5. camp
3. cap	

Page 47
Circle the following pictures: fish, pig, lips, mitten, witch, six, pin, Indian.

Page 48
Color the following pictures: person who is sick, pig, six, man, and zipper.

Page 49
1. fish	5. bill	9. pill
2. bib	6. ring	10. sit
3. kid	7. pin	11. dig
4. kiss	8. tick	12. win

Page 50
Across
2. rib	5. fish	6. mitt

Down
1. pin	3. hill	4. gift

Page 51
1. pig	4. milk
2. big	5. kiss
3. hill	

Page 52
The following should be colored purple: every letter a, fan, cap, band, ax, bat.
The following should be colored green: every letter i, lid, pin, crib, swim, wig.

Page 53
Circle the following pictures: pumpkin, sun, duck, cup, mummy, tub, rug, people hugging.

Page 54
1. mug	5. sub	9. muff
2. tub	6. cut	10. mud
3. bug	7. pup	11. gull
4. up	8. tuck	12. hut

Page 55
Color the following pictures: people tugging, duck, scissors cutting, gum, bud.

Page 56

b	d	r	k
u	r	u	g
s	u	n	u
n	m	u	m
h	u	t	x

Page 57
1. pup	3. sun	5. tub
2. bus	4. mud	

Page 58
The following pictures should be connected: umbrella, mix, bud, pan, van, cut, pants, stick, sun, dig. The final picture should be a star.

Page 59
Circle the following pictures: fox, stop sign, doll, clock, octopus, sock, top, box, dog.

Page 60
The letter o should be in the middle of all words. Check to make sure the pictures are correctly matched.

Page 61
1. log	4. dog	7. pot
2. fox	5. mop	8. cot
3. box	6. dot	

Answer Key

Page 62
All words should be filled in with letter o.

Page 63
1. lock
2. cob
3. doll
4. frog

Page 64
1. u
2. a
3. i
4. o
5. i
6. u
7. a
8. u
9. o

Page 65
Circle the following pictures: bed, eggs, net, desk, vest, dress, bread, web, elf, tent.

Page 66
1. web
2. hen
3. sled
4. pen
5. net
6. bed
7. ten
8. bell
9. jet
10. men
11. nest
12. belt

Page 67
The letter e should be in the middle of all words. Check to make sure lines are drawn to the correct picture.

Page 68

e	l	e	p	h	a	n	t
l	h	t	e	n	t	e	e
f	e	e	t	h	e	a	d
w	e	t	s	e	l	e	g
e	p	e	n	e	h	e	n

Page 69
1. wet
2. elf
3. pen
4. tent
5. Eggs
6. jet

Page 70
a – Circle apple, alligator, and bat.
i – Circle fish, pin, and person swimming.
e – Circle desk, net, and bed.
u – Circle truck, cup, and rug.
o – Circle dog, clock, and mop.

Page 71
1. r, g
2. b, b
3. c, t
4. d, g
5. s, n
6. b, g
7. t, n
8. m, p
9. f, n
10. n, t
11. p, n
12. t, p
13. b, x
14. b, d
15. f, n
16. r, n

Page 72
1. cat
2. sick
3. vet
4. shot
5. hug
6. Answers will vary.

Page 73
lips—i
tent—e
box—o
cup or mug—u
cat—a
apple—a
duck—u
pig—i
fox—o
bed—e

Page 74
1. cat
2. hat
3. sun
4. dog
5. frog
6. fish

Page 76
Circle baby, radio, cane, grapes, vase, snake, angel, rake.

Page 77
1. cane
2. cake
3. gate
4. race
5. day
6. vase
7. bake
8. base
9. face
10. lake
11. play
12. tape

Page 78
Color the following pieces of mail: case/lace, pain/Zane, dame/flame, nail/pail, sail/jail, take/fake, date/wait, May/say.

Page 79
Draw a line from the following words: rain, tail, ate, tame, lay, rake, vase, take, cape, pace, May, hail, make, cake, tape, fame.

Page 80
1. Jake
2. race
3. lake
4. rain
5. day

Page 81
Circle the following pictures: pie, kite, spider, tire, bike, nine, lion, fire, dime.

Page 82
1. kite
2. mice
3. vine
4. pine
5. tie
6. ice
7. time
8. fire
9. hive
10. wire
11. dice
12. hike

Page 83
Color the following kites: dime/time, nine/dine, bike/like, side/tide, kite/bite, hire/tire, line/fine.

Page 84
Check to make sure pictures match words.

x	l	i	m	e
d	i	m	e	n
i	n	a	z	i
v	e	b	x	n
e	p	i	n	e

Page 85
1. kite
2. fine
3. mine
4. five
5. time

Page 86
1. long
2. long
3. short
4. long
5. short
6. long
7. long
8. short
9. short

Page 87
Circle the following pictures: unicorn, calendar with June, ruler, glue, unicycle, mule, suit, cube.

Page 88
1. glue
2. tube
3. Luke
4. dude
5. cube
6. June
7. fruit
8. flute
9. ruler
10. dune
11. Duke
12. tune

Page 89
Circle the following pieces of fruit: June/dune, fruit/suit, tube/cube, mule/rule, cute/lute, true/blue, dude/rude, Luke/Duke.

Page 90

Across	Down
1. suit	1. Sue
3. tube	2. June
5. Duke	4. mule

Page 91
1. Sue
2. glue
3. June
4. flute
5. tune

Page 92
a – snake, rain, base, ate
i – pine, ride, ripe, fine
u – tube, cute, dude, jute

Page 93
The correct path is as follows: nose, rope, coat, soap, bow, snow, boat.

Page 94
1. long
2. short
3. short
4. long
5. long
6. short
7. short
8. long
9. short
10. long
11. long
12. long
13. long
14. short
15. long
16. long

Page 95
1. rope
2. boat
3. goat
4. robe
5. note
6. soap
7. nose
8. cold
9. bone
10. hose
11. road
12. cone

Page 96
Check to make sure pictures match directions.

Page 97
1. goat
2. toe
3. note
4. row
5. snow
6. rope

Page 98
Match the following pictures: coat/soap, suit/glue, rain/apron, slide/iron, mule/fruit, train/cane, ice/lion, goat/rope.

Page 99
Circle the following pictures: feet, zebra, tea, person sleeping, bee, seal, tree, eagle, key, three, leaf.

Page 100
Make sure all pictures match up with correct words.

Page 101
1. pea
2. meat
3. seal
4. eat
5. heat
6. east
7. eel
8. tree
9. sea
10. bee
11. three
12. feet

Page 102
1. ee
2. ee
3. ee
4. e
5. ee
6. e
7. ee
8. e
9. ee
10. e

Page 103
bee—three, free, tree, me, wee
weed—tweed, bead, seed, heed, need
meat—Pete, feat, beet, heat, beat
peek—sneak, freak, meek, reek

Page 104
1. a
2. a
3. o
4. e
5. i
6. o
7. u
8. i
9. e
10. o
11. a
12. e
13. u
14. i
15. u

Page 105
Circle the following pictures: bike, sheep, remote, person writing, lake, cube.

Page 106
1. boat
2. kite
3. cube
4. toe
5. cake
6. three
7. rake

Page 107
1. o
2. a
3. i
4. u
5. i
6. e
7. a
8. a

Page 108
1. sheep
2. grapes
3. kite
4. mule
5. goat
6. crate
7. bee
8. eat

Page 110
1. Color fruit and frog the same. Color dress and drum the same.
2. Color train and truck the same. Color bricks and brush the same.
3. Color pretzel and princess the same. Color grapes and grasshopper the same.
4. Color bread and bride the same. Color crane and crib the same.

Page 111
1. cry
2. truck
3. grin
4. track
5. prince
6. fruit
7. crab
8. grapes
9. train
10. brush
11. crane
12. drop

Page 112
1. gr
2. pr
3. tr
4. br
5. pr
6. dr
7. fr
8. br

Page 113
1. dr—dragon, dress, drum
2. fr—frame, frog, fries

Page 114
1. Circle flamingo, flag, flame.
2. Circle cloud, cliff, clock.
3. Circle blocks, blouse, blanket.
4. Circle plane, plug, planets.
5. Circle glass, glue, glove.

Answer Key

Page 115
Color the following petals: club, flag, globe, black, play, plant.

Page 116
1. plum   5. clam   9. plate
2. glove   6. clown   10. clap
3. flame   7. flute   11. blocks
4. blouse 8. globe   12. flower

Page 117
1. pl   3. pl   5. fl
2. bl   4. cl   6. fl

Page 118
1. Circle square and squid.
2. Circle spill and spoon.
3. Circle star and stop sign.
4. Circle skunk and skip.
5. Circle person sleeping and sled.

Page 119
1. ski   5. stamp   9. stump
2. nest   6. smoke   10. swim
3. sled   7. swing   11. sponge
4. slide   8. star   12. spaghetti

Page 120
1. desk   3. spoon   5. nest
2. skate   4. skunk

Page 121

s p i d e r s s
s s s e s s k s
t o a s t k u p
s s s k u y n o
s l u g m s k o
s c o r p i o n

Page 122
1. mp   6. mp   11. mp
2. sk   7. sk   12. mp
3. sk   8. mp   13. mp
4. mp   9. mp   14. sk
5. mp   10. mp   15. mp

Page 123
Stories will vary.

Page 124
1. Circle nest and vest.
2. Circle toast and fist.
3. Circle tank and sink.
4. Circle wink and bank.

Page 125
1. nest   5. bunk   9. vest
2. bank   6. rink   10. think
3. list   7. wink   11. fast
4. coast   8. sink   12. west

Page 126
1. Color the picture of the wing.
2. Color the picture of the person singing.
3. Color the picture of the ring.
4. Color the picture of the king.
5. Color the picture of the swing.

Page 127
1. king   4. swing   6. string
2. spring 5. sing   7. sting
3. ring

Page 128
Every missing letter should be filled in with the letter y.

Page 129
1. spy   4. fry   6. fly
2. sky   5. July   7. pony
3. cry

Page 130
candy—handy, Mandy, dandy
spy—fly, my, spry, by, buy, cry, try, bye
sky—fry, pry, retry, ply, why, try
lady—baby, penny, buggy, lazy

Page 131
1. cry   2. fly   3. pony   4. July

Page 132
king—Circle swing, ring, wing.
bump—Circle stamp, person jumping, lamp.
test—Circle nest, toast, ghost.
flask—Circle tusk, mask, desk.
wink—Circle sink, person thinking, and person drinking.

Page 133
1. Down: plug, Across: plus
2. Down: flag, Across: fly
3. Down: snow, Across: snake
4. Down: bride, Across: broom
5. Down: fries, Across: frog

Page 134
sl—slippers and person sleeping
gl—glove and globe
gr—grandma and grapes
fl—flowers and flag
cl—clock and cloud
bl—block and blender

Page 135
The path is as follows: star, tree, drum, fly, clown, stamp, flag, plug, sled, clock, globe, fries, blocks, snow, pretzel, stop sign.

Page 136
1. nk   4. st   7. st   9. sk
2. sk   5. lk   8. st   10. st
3. st   6. mp

Page 137
st—best, vest, story
pl—plane, play, please, plow
gl—glove, gland, glow
lk—milk, silk, sulk, bilk, bulk

Page 138
1. my   3. crown   5. clock
2. marry   4. king   6. start

Page 139
1. fl   4. gl   7. cl
2. sp   5. Fl   8. sp
3. br   6. sp   9. pl

Page 140
1. desk   5. baby   9. glass
2. cry   6. sled   10. fairy
3. swim   7. bunk   11. king
4. plug   8. skate   12. tree

Page 142
1. float   3. rob   5. mail
2. melt   4. glue   6. shave

Page 143
1. play   3. swim   5. cook
2. walk   4. run   6. sing

Page 144
–ed—jumped, snowed, rained cooked, mailed
–ing—jumping, snowing, raining, cooking, mailing

Page 145
1. looking   3. lived   5. playing
2. opened   4. studied 6. cooking

Page 146
Color the sections with the following pictures: thimble, three, thread, thirteen, thermometer, person thinking, person throwing, thumb.

Page 147
Color the following wheel sections: whistle, wheat, wheelbarrow, whale, wheelchair.

Page 148

q a w h a l e
x t h r e a d
w h e e l x u
u r a s p k c
d o t h r e e
i w m w b x j

Page 149
1. wheel   3. whale   5. whistle
2. thorn   4. think   6. thimble

Page 150
1. shark   5. shuttle   8. shade
2. wash   6. fish   9. sheep
3. sharp   7. shop   10. shower
4. shot

Page 151
The letters sh should be filled in each word.

Page 152
The letters ch should be filled in each word and twice in church.

Page 153
1. lunch   3. chicken   5. chair
2. cheese   4. cherries

Page 154
1. kn   3. n   5. kn
2. kn   4. kn   6. n

Page 155
The path is as follows: knife, knack, knew, knee, knot, knave, knead, know, knob, knight, knit.

Page 156
The path is as follows: chick, wheel, sheep, thermometer, chain, cheese, wheelbarrow, shoe, chair, whistle, shark, chin, thirteen, wheelchair, thimble, ship, cherries.

Page 157
knight—knife, knot
teeth—thief, thread
whistle—wheel, whale
ship—shark, shower
chain—cheeks, cherries

Page 158
sh—short, shout, push, gush, shelf
ch—chart, chick, chin

wh—what, whale
th—thread, path, math, tooth, thing

Page 159
1. knife   3. whistle   5. shoes
2. gnaw   4. thief   6. chess

Page 160
1. sheep   3. teeth   5. chair
2. knot   4. whistle   6. chick

Page 161
th—throat, throne, thug, thing, thank
ch—chain, crunch, cherry, chair, chocolate
wh—whittle, whack, why, whine
–ed—played, stored, walked, fished, danced
–ing—jumping, rowing, chasing, running

Page 162
Stories will vary.

Page 163
Color the following balloons: I'll, they're, can't, she's, it'll, I'm, we'll, it's, doesn't, you're.

Page 164
he's = he is
it's = it is
she's = she is
you'll = you will
I'll = I will
he'll = he will
won't = will not
doesn't = does not
can't = cannot
they're = they are
we're = we are
I'm = I am

Page 165
1. It's   2. He's   3. She's   4. It's

Page 166
1. I'm   3. They're
2. You're   4. We're

Page 167
1. can't   3. doesn't
2. isn't   4. won't

Page 168
1. I'll   3. She'll   5. We'll
2. He'll   4. You'll   6. It'll

Page 169
The path is as follows: can't, doesn't, I'll, they're, it's, don't, isn't, you're, it's, he'll, won't, she's

Page 170
–ing—jumping, sinking, dancing, playing, singing, reading
–ed—painted, talked, skated, rained, hunted, raked
contractions—it'll, you're, we'll, isn't, he's, she'll

Page 171
1. thirty   5. sheep   9. whip
2. wheat   6. think   10. knock
3. knee   7. knife   11. church
4. chips   8. cherry 12. throne

Page 172
1. We're eating candy.
2. The bunny hopped away.
3. The clothes are drying.
4. We're making popcorn.
5. He's riding a horse.
6. He tugged on the rope.